Classroom Management

Classroom Management

Authentic Experiences in Classroom Teaching

Jacqueline G. Van Schooneveld
and Michael Ryan

ROWMAN & LITTLEFIELD
Lanham • Boulder • New York • London

Published by Rowman & Littlefield
An imprint of The Rowman & Littlefield Publishing Group, Inc.
4501 Forbes Boulevard, Suite 200, Lanham, Maryland 20706
www.rowman.com

86-90 Paul Street, London EC2A 4NE, United Kingdom

Copyright © 2023 by Jacqueline G. Van Schooneveld and Michael Ryan

All rights reserved. No part of this book may be reproduced in any form or by any electronic or mechanical means, including information storage and retrieval systems, without written permission from the publisher, except by a reviewer who may quote passages in a review.

British Library Cataloguing in Publication Information Available

Library of Congress Cataloging-in-Publication Data

Names: Van Schooneveld, Jacqueline G., author. | Ryan, Michael, 1971– author.
Title: Classroom management: authentic experiences in classroom teaching / Jacqueline G. Van Schooneveld and Michael Ryan.
Description: Lanham, Maryland: Rowman & Littlefield, 2023. | Summary: "This book is written to be an engaging and interactive text forcing teacher candidates to reflect, apply, create and question what they would do in a variety of situations"—Provided by publisher.
Identifiers: LCCN 2023007451 (print) | LCCN 2023007452 (ebook) | ISBN 9781475866155 (cloth) | ISBN 9781475866162 (paperback) | ISBN 9781475866179 (epub)
Subjects: LCSH: Classroom management. | Classroom environment. | Motivation in education. | School discipline. | Parent-teacher relationships.
Classification: LCC LB3013 .V25 2023 (print) | LCC LB3013 (ebook) | DDC 371.102/4—dc23/eng/20230223
LC record available at https://lccn.loc.gov/2023007451
LC ebook record available at https://lccn.loc.gov/2023007452

This book is dedicated to all aspiring teachers and current teachers. To their incredible dedication to this challenging but rewarding profession, and to their dedication for creating warm, safe, and positive learning environments for all students.

Special thanks to my family Andrew, Jameson, and Olivia, and my parents Frances and Howard for their love and support throughout the writing process.
—J. Van Schooneveld

Heartfelt thanks go out to my husband Kevin, my son Noah, and my Mom Claudia for always being my cheerleaders and supporting my passion for teaching and learning.
—M. Ryan

Contents

Acknowledgments — ix

Introduction: The Method Behind the Madness — xi

Chapter 1: Building Your Philosophy — 1

Chapter 2: Engaging and Motivating Learners — 9

Chapter 3: Rules and Discipline — 25

Chapter 4: Procedures — 43

Chapter 5: Designing the Physical Classroom — 59

Chapter 6: Collaborating with Families — 77

Chapter 7: Self-Care: Managing Yourself — 93

Acknowledgments

Special acknowledgment to Amy Austin, Kristen Cheney, Dana DeMinico, Amanda DiPasqua, Frances Flicker, Christine Hindman, Bronwyn Lakowski, Meredith Miller, Theresa Pignatro Christine Prestianne, Patrick Ricci, and Lindsay Sutton. These experienced teachers contributed to the "Teacher Talk" sections throughout the book. They provided valuable suggestions and practical ideas for how some of these concepts of classroom management are implemented in the classroom.

We want to acknowledge our former students at West Chester University who took our courses on classroom management. These students challenged us to give them authentic experiences to learn about and apply ideas of classroom management. They engaged in many of the activities described throughout this book, and provided feedback about what else they wanted to learn and experience. Their work and questions throughout class made us think critically about providing authentic experiences and were the inspiration to write this book.

Finally, we would like to acknowledge our colleagues at West Chester University who supported and encouraged us, and many of whom acted as critical friends throughout this process.

Introduction

The Method Behind the Madness

"Though this be madness, yet there is method in't" (Hamlet Act 2, Scene 2). A line so eloquently projected by Polonius in Shakespeare's *Hamlet*. Polonius explained that while Hamlet's behavior might seem absurd to onlookers, there was good intent and thoughtfulness behind Hamlet's actions.

While wearing various hats and juggling multiple balls, teachers are creating classroom environments to accommodate the needs of a diverse set of learners. Experienced teachers do this seamlessly. Think of the classroom as a ballet. The teacher and students are all engaged in this ballet, with simultaneous leaps, jumps, lifts, and turns. Someone might think it is madness to have all this happening concurrently, yet no one collides, and everyone executes his or her part.

Think of a ballet as a teacher's classroom management. To an outsider, it might look like organized chaos. Students going everywhere, doing different things. Yet in a beautifully synced classroom, all students seem to know exactly what to do, and where to go. Additionally, all students recognize the importance of their role in helping ensure that the classroom is a friendly, welcoming, and productive place. We call this a beautiful classroom ballet.

An observer might not see how the teacher thought through every piece of choreography, so that students can realize their roles and teacher expectations. They may not recognize that the teacher held numerous rehearsals where the class worked out kinks and challenges to get to the point where everyone in the room was moving together in harmony. The outside observer only sees a beautiful ballet.

An aspiring or novice teacher might see the beautiful classroom ballet but does not know how the teacher designed and implemented the choreography, class rehearsals, and made professional decisions that contributed to the success of the classroom ballet. The knowledge and skills needed to cultivate an effective classroom management system can be learned through reading professional resources, talking with other teachers, and lots and lots of practice.

Novice teachers are often challenged by seeing the final ballet without the advantage of understanding the method behind the performance. Lortie (1975) coined the term *apprenticeship of observation* to describe how preservice and novice teachers oftentimes imitate or replicate what they observed teachers doing when they were K–12 students.

Preservice and novice teachers sometimes mimic teacher practices that they have experienced or seen. While this might appear an effective way to learn, teachers should realize that people have different personalities and philosophies. These differences can drive how they run and manage their classrooms. Additionally, every class has its own personality and needs. Adjustments to practices in order to accommodate different and diverse groups of children are necessary. Teachers must be flexible, critical thinkers, and creative problem solvers in order to develop classroom management skills, not mimickers.

Classroom management and behavior issues are one of the biggest struggles of preservice or novice teachers (Postholm, 2013). Taking the time to learn more about classroom management techniques, ways to cultivate a positive and collaborative classroom climate, as well as methods of dealing with discipline challenges helps teachers better prepare for their work with students. As preservice or novice teachers gain in their understanding and confidence in classroom management, they develop a philosophy and vision for their classrooms. They construct a framework that will help them to develop the structures and procedures critical to establish a classroom environment that will support the growth and development of all students.

Readers of this book will understand that classroom management is a term that encompasses the relationships teachers form with their students, communities created in classrooms, procedures needed to ensure that students can engage in learning effectively, ways that teachers structure lessons and learning opportunities, connections formed with students' families, and ways to deal with behavioral challenges. Developing and producing the classroom ballet takes planning, understanding, experimentation, focus, and effort.

Providing authentic experiences for novice teachers is paramount to developing a deeper knowledge and understanding of classroom management. This book is designed to engage you in challenging activities that will initiate critical thinking, develop your own philosophy for classroom management, and apply those ideas to practical experiences.

Each chapter begins with foundational information related to each chapter topic. Understanding the research and rationale behind the ideas and practices helps teachers to discern its importance and effectiveness.

After providing foundational information, you, as the reader, will engage in different activities. These activities will challenge you to apply that foundational knowledge and bring in your own experiences to work through the activities. There is a section called "Teacher Talk," in which expert teachers share their knowledge about the topic and provide some tips and tricks they find helpful in their classrooms. Finally, each chapter ends with an "It's Your Turn to Create" section. In these sections, you will begin to create something you can use in your own classroom or future classroom.

This book is designed to be interactive and give you authentic experiences that will build your classroom management toolbox so that you can create a beautiful classroom ballet.

REFERENCES

Lortie, D. C. (2007). *Schoolteacher a sociological study*. University of Chicago Press.

Postholm, M. B. (2013). Classroom management: What does research tell us? *European Educational Research Journal, 12*(3), 389–402.

Chapter 1

Building Your Philosophy

We all have different and specific reasons for wanting to become teachers. Somewhere embedded in all our "whys" is the opportunity to help support children as they learn to move toward their hopes and dreams in life. We hold a vision of our classroom environment's actualities and possibilities. We use this vision as a goal that we want to attain and achieve for our students.

Rooted in this vision lies a set of beliefs that informs an individual's work and creates a philosophy that guides his/her actions and decisions as a teacher. Ideally, this philosophy is cultivated as educators learn more about students, create an environment for learning, and examine how they see and interpret their students' behaviors and habits.

Philosophies grow and change as teachers gain experience, learn more information, and communicate with other professionals. Teachers' philosophies impact their decisions and how they interact with students. It is critical that teachers take time to examine and reflect on their beliefs and philosophies. This will enable the teacher to be well informed on how they "see" students and the "why" that underpins the things that they do (Postholm, 2013; Smith & Lambert, 2008). This chapter will provide you with an overview of research and concepts you will want to consider as you develop your classroom management philosophy.

RESEARCH AND CLASSROOM MANAGEMENT

There was little concern and research about classroom management prior to the 1950s. Those who did dabble in research peripherally related to classroom management often explored topics in psychology and psychiatry as their primary goal. Early research by Fritz Redl and William Wattenberg taught us how a group impacts everyone's behavior, noting that group members take on specific roles that influence how they act (Charles, 2008). Additionally, Redl and Wattenberg talked about roles that students expect teachers to fill as part of classroom life (Charles, 2008).

As research continued to expand, we learned more about the factors that impact behavior and effective classroom management methods. Burrhus Frederick Skinner noted how individuals could shape behaviors by using reinforcements for desired behaviors and implementing behavior modifications (Charles, 2008; Wiseman & Hunt, 2013).

Lee and Marlene Canter (1976) built on this through their concept of assertive discipline. In this approach, they differentiated between positive and negative consequences, helping to guide children to make better choices (Canter & Canter, 1976; Charles, 2008; Wiseman & Hunt, 2013). They stressed that classroom environments needed to support students' right to learn and teachers' right to teach (Canter & Canter, 1976; Charles, 2008; Wiseman & Hunt, 2013). Canter and Canter noted that behaviors should be dealt with quickly and calmly and that there should be a hierarchy of consequences that were known to the children (Canter & Canter, 1976; Charles, 2008; Wiseman & Hunt, 2013). Researchers do not all agree on what makes a consequence effective.

Other research focused on the importance of creating a classroom community for and with students. Rudolph Dreikurs' (1969) work illuminated the need for children to feel a sense of belonging in the classroom. This work highlighted the benefits of creating a democratic classroom where the students and the teacher have a say in creating rules and discussing consequences, and giving students some say in academics (Dreikurs, 1969; Charles, 2008; Charney, 2002; Denton, 2005; Wiseman & Hunt, 2013).

Taking the time to identify, teach, and review routines, expectations, and rules help to create a solid structure that supports student success in the classroom (Canter & Canter, 1976; Glasser, 1992; Kohn, 1993; 2006). Alfie Kohn's (1993; 2006) work, along with the work of the Center for Responsive Schools (Charney, 2002; Denton, 2005), elaborate on the importance of community as a tool to involve students actively in establishing the rules and norms for the classroom.

Classroom meetings are used as key vehicles for talking about, making decisions about, and processing behavioral or interpersonal challenges in school (Charles, 2008; Charney, 2002; Wiseman & Hunt, 2013). In these types of classrooms, the teachers are not "in charge" of everything. They facilitate the work with the goal of helping students to learn effective ways of behaving in a community. Taking this stance gives students a sense of some power over the classroom and decisions. Students also learn that with power comes a great deal of responsibility to help cultivate and maintain an open, welcoming, understanding, and friendly community. The goal is to develop students as caring, solid, and productive citizens of the world.

Establishing an effective learning community requires solid and trusting relationships among everyone in the classroom. Teachers need to see their classrooms as social systems they develop and maintain (Charney, 2002; Kohn, 1993; 2006; Postholm, 2013; Kohn, 1993; 2006). As teachers support these systems, they must be aware of and tend to students' different physical, social, and emotional needs (Charney, 2002; Dreikurs, 1969; Kohn, 1993; 2006). Doing this will help create a classroom where teachers foster positive social interactions among all community members (Charney, 2002; Kohn, 1993; 2006; Postholm, 2013).

Educators who are able to create effective communities foster social systems where students feel comfortable and have a sense that their needs are being met (Charney, 2002; Dreikurs, 1969; Postholm, 2013; Tate, 2007). Teachers must first critically examine their thoughts and beliefs about students (Charney, 2002; Glasser, 1992; Gordon, 1991; Kohn 1993; 2006; Postholm, 2013; Smith & Lambert, 2008). Deep-seated biases and beliefs impact how teachers view and treat students, ultimately influencing how teachers teach and run their classrooms (Charney, 2002; Glasser, 1992; Gordon, 1991; Kohn, 1993; 2006; Postholm, 2013; Smith & Lambert, 2008).

Students form beliefs and impressions about their teachers based on how they experience teachers' actions and reactions in and out of the classroom (Postholm, 2013; Smith & Lambert, 2008; Tate, 2007). Brain research suggests that students must like and respect their teachers in order to cultivate positive and trusting relationships with them (Tate, 2007). Addressing biases and beliefs helps teachers to remain open to looking at students through a positive lens rather than focusing on their shortcomings (Postholm, 2013; Smith & Lambert, 2008).

When teachers can acknowledge the positive qualities of their students, they are open to examining students' behaviors to identify and try to address the underlying causes for certain reactions (Charney, 2002; Dreikurs, 1969; Smith & Lambert, 2008). Teachers need to cultivate their social and emotional intelligence to support effective interactions in the classroom that will allow them to be positive models for their students (Ginott, 1971; Postholm, 2013).

Teachers' lessons, reactions, decisions, and responses can support or hinder effective classroom management. Jacob Kounin (1970) noted that it was important for educators to have what he called "withitness." This means that teachers must be aware of everything happening in all parts of the classroom. Kounin (1970), William Glasser, Alfie Kohn (1993; 2006), and the Center for Responsive Schools (Charney, 2002; Denton, 2005) also emphasize the role instruction plays in maintaining good classroom management (Kounin, 1970).

Lessons must actively engage students from the beginning to the end and help them understand why what they are learning is so important. There should also be opportunities for students to have a say in what they are learning or exploring, tapping into students' interests (Charney, 2002; Denton, 2005; Kohn, 1993; 2006; Kounin, 1970; Glasser, 1992). Additionally, teachers need to support smooth transitions between lessons to maintain students' focus and help foster understanding.

Additional research focuses on how teachers respond to misbehavior and teaching students how to behave properly. As noted earlier, students form opinions of their teachers based on how teachers speak and act in the classroom (Postholm, 2013; Smith & Lambert, 2008; Tate, 2007).

The language we use matters. The work of Haim Ginott (1971), Thomas Gordon (1991), and the Center for Responsive Schools (Charney, 2002; Denton, 2015) notes the importance of using specific types of language to communicate clearly and effectively, and when necessary, firmly with students. They note that "I messages" are very effective tools for communicating feelings or frustration without finger-pointing or assigning blame. It is crucial to start with language that tries to influence students to act appropriately before firmly correcting or disciplining them for misbehavior (Charney, 2002; Denton, 2015; Ginott, 1971; Kohn, 1993; 2006).

In order to help students learn prosocial behavior, research suggests that teachers need to act as role models as well as take the time to teach students proper behaviors and problem-solving skills explicitly (Canter & Canter, 1976; Charney, 2002; Denton, 2015; Ginott, 1971; Kohn, 1993; 2006). The focus is on helping students learn to be better citizens of the classroom community, rather than simply telling students what they have done wrong.

Teaching can and should occur at the beginning of the year to develop students' understanding of classroom expectations (Canter & Canter, 1976; Charney, 2002). Additionally, teachers should take time to revisit these skills when necessary or address a specific skill that has presented as a challenge to the class. Ultimately these types of prosocial skills will help students at school, at home, and in life (Canter & Canter, 1976; Charney, 2002; Denton, 2015; Kohn, 1993; 2006).

Research on effective classroom management is ongoing. All research impacts the knowledge about effective ways to work with and support students. For example, in recent years, there has been a focus on the impact of trauma on children and ways schools can support students by employing trauma-informed practices (National Child Traumatic Stress Network, 2008; Wiest-Stevenson & Lee, 2016). This work has helped to foster an understating of why students may act or react in certain ways in our classrooms.

Educators are continuously learning from research and should continue to stay abreast of this information to best support their understanding of their students and effective ways to support student learning in the classroom. Research provides a framework on which teachers can start to construct and communicate their philosophy of classroom management.

Developing Your Philosophy

Everything teachers learn impacts their work with students. Effective teachers synthesize their understanding of research and practical information to help them create an outline explaining the "why" behind the ways they teach, interact with students, and run their classrooms. Ultimately, as teachers formulate their classroom management philosophy, they are looking to answer the question, "What do you believe is important in order to have effective classroom management?" A well-developed philosophy of classroom management is grounded in theory and provides the support necessary to guide a teacher's work in the classroom.

As teachers are working toward answering this question, it is crucial that they take time to examine any biases and beliefs that may influence the ways they might see, act toward, or speak to their students. We know students react to how their teachers interact with them and manage the class.

As you will explore in greater depth in chapter 2, classrooms need to be places where all students feel welcome, wanted, and worthy. This begins with the teacher taking an honest and objective look at the ways they create an environment that embraces all students or not. This is challenging work as it causes individuals to confront deeply entrenched beliefs, many of which can subconsciously impact how they interact with certain students or groups of students in their classrooms. Many resources can help to inform and facilitate this work. Table 1.1 provides some suggestions that will help individuals start to examine and identify any biases that may impact their work with students.

There is no "correct" way to craft or record a philosophy of classroom management. It ultimately should help teachers effectively communicate what they believe, what they would do, and why these are criucial to support student learning. An effective philosophy should address the following: creating an environment for all; communication, instruction, and engagement; and classroom rules and discipline. These will all be addressed in greater depth in the remaining chapters of this book. However, we encourage readers to start drafting a philosophy using the chart provided (table 1.1).

A teacher's philosophy will continue to take shape through their personal and professional experiences. As readers work through the book's next

Table 1.1. Your philosophy for creating a positive learning environment

My beliefs about all students . . .	Ways to establish and support an environment for all . . .	My beliefs about teaching and learning . . .	My thoughts on establishing classroom structures and discipline . . .

chapters, they should continually revisit, modify, and expand their answers from this table.

In the following chapters, readers will continue to learn about different domains associated with classroom management, engage in various activities, hear from different expert teachers, and apply their understanding of the domains to create their own classroom management practices. As you do this work, it is important to return to your philosophy and use that as a foundation. Remember, your philosophies and beliefs will be reflected in your classroom. Our goal is to graduate global citizens who will be caring, productive, and construct a positive social community.

REFERENCES

Canter, L. with Canter, M. 1976. Assertive discipline: A take-charge approach for today's educator: Santa Monica, CA: Canter and Associates.

Charles, C. (2008). *Building classroom discipline* (9th ed.). Boston: Allyn & Bacon.

Charney, R. (2002). *Teaching children to care: Classroom management for ethical and academic growth, K–8*. Center for Responsive Schools, Inc.

Denton, P. (2005). *Learning through academic choice*. Northeast Foundation for Children.

Denton, P. (2015). The power of our words: Teacher language that helps children learn. Center for Responsive Schools, Inc.

Dreikurs, R. (1969). *Dynamics of classroom behavior: Education in-service: Twelve 30-minute lessons*. University of Nebraska, Great Plains National ITV Library.

Ginott, H. (1971). *Teacher and child*. New York: Macmillan.

Glasser, William. 1992. *The quality school: Managing students without coercion*. Second, expanded ed. New York: HarperPerennial.

Gordon, T. (1991). *Discipline that works: Promoting self-discipline in children*. Penguin.

Kohn, A. (1993). *Punished by rewards: The trouble with gold stars, incentive plans, A's, praise, and other bribes*. New York: Houghton Mifflin.

Kohn, A. (2006). *Beyond discipline: From compliance to community*. ASCD.

Kounin, J. S. (1970). *Discipline and group management in classrooms*. Holt, Rinehart & Winston.

National Child Traumatic Stress Network (NCTSN). (2008). *Child trauma toolkit for educators*.

Postholm, M. B. (2013). Classroom management: What does research tell us?. *European Educational Research Journal, 12*(3), 389–402.

Smith, R., & Lambert, M. (2008). Assuming the best. *Educational Leadership, 66*(1), 16–21.

Tate, M. L. (2007). *Shouting won't grow dendrites: 20 techniques for managing a brain-compatible classroom.* Corwin Press.

Wiest-Stevenson, C., & Lee, C. (2016). Trauma-informed schools. *Journal of Evidence-Informed Social Work, 13*(5), 498–503.

Wiseman, D. G., & Hunt, G. H. (2013). *Best practice in motivation and management in the classroom.* Charles C. Thomas Publisher.

Chapter 2

Engaging and Motivating Learners

Good classroom management is focused on instruction that provides opportunities for all students to learn and be successful (Wong et al., 2018). As teachers strive to create an environment conducive to students' learning, they must look carefully at ways that the classroom is a welcoming space where learning opportunities fully engage students and motivate them to try new and challenging things. This chapter explores strategies teachers can use to develop classroom environments that embrace all students and instructional techniques that will support and promote student learning.

FOUNDATION

All students need to feel safe, welcome, and wanted. Students can sense this from the moment they meet their teacher and enter the classroom. Every classroom is filled with interactions that create dynamic relationships between the teacher and students as well as among the students (Danielson, 2013; Postholm, 2013). Teachers' interactions with students should help cultivate a sense of respect for their students and a rapport that communicates genuine care and concern for the students (Danielson, 2013).

Taking time to establish this environment with and among students cultivates a sense of safety and belonging that helps meet each student's basic needs and allows them to be ready and available for learning (Maslow & Frager, 1987; Dreikurs, 1969). This helps to foster an environment where students feel that they can trust their teacher. Trust is crucial to having students be willing to tune in to classroom instruction (Wong et al., 2018). Teachers need to have solid social and emotional competence (Postholm, 2013).

Creating a welcoming environment also means recognizing how all students are seen and represented in the classroom. Teachers need to acknowledge the ways that culture influences how students interact in the classroom. Educators must develop a solid level of cultural competence to be prepared for today's diverse classrooms and schools (Weinstein, Tomlinson-Clarke, Curran, 2004). Teachers need to cultivate practices that "speak to the essence of who students are" (Milner et al., 2019, p. 24).

Teachers must "recognize that we are all cultural beings, with our own beliefs, biases, and assumptions about human behavior" (Weinstein, Tomlinson-Clarke, & Curran, 2003, p. 270). This requires individuals to recognize their own egocentrism and biases, noting how they may impact or hinder developing a classroom environment that welcomes all students (Weinstein et al., 2003; 2004).

After critically reviewing the culture and environment, teachers need to take the time to develop a knowledge of students' cultural backgrounds, cultivate an awareness of the broader context of their students' lives, commit to employing strategies that are culturally aligned, and commit to fostering a caring classroom community where all students are embraced (Weinstein et al., 2004). The goal should be to create an environment that embraces a multicultural stance as well as work to create equitable learning spaces for students (Gorski & Swalwell, 2015).

Establishing a caring and inclusive environment that promotes positive relationships with and among students helps to ensure that students feel safe and sets the tone for learning. The time we take to establish relationships with our students helps to cultivate a community. Marzano (2017) notes that students' state of mind is a mediating factor in student learning but adds that teachers need to use effective instructional strategies to maximize student engagement.

Careful attention must be paid to instructional decisions to help engage students as learners and keep them tuned into the essential skills or strategies presented during a given lesson (Jensen, 2005; Marzano, 2017). This requires that teachers plan lessons carefully, focusing on ways to thoughtfully group and present material to develop meaning and understanding (Jensen, 2005; Johnson, Uline, & Perez, 2019; Marzano, 2017). Teachers must be deliberate about their instructional decisions to engage and support all learners (Johnson, Uline, & Perez, 2019; Marzano, 2017). Additionally, teachers must consider how they can support academic success and link learning opportunities to students' communities and cultures (Ladson-Billings, 1995).

PUTTING IDEAS INTO PRACTICE

We all dream of creating wildly engaging learning opportunities where all students will be completely enthralled in every lesson. This is not something that develops simply by making every lesson "fun." Engaging students starts with taking time to invest in relationships with each student at the start of the year and supporting the creation of a strong classroom community. This work begins before students step foot into the classroom.

Effective teachers find ways of reaching out to students and establishing a connection a few weeks before the start of the school year. Often teachers will send a welcome note specifically to the students introducing themselves. Sometimes, students will be asked to prepare or bring something on the first day of school that will help everyone get to know one another. Additionally, teachers might send these notes out as videos giving the students an opportunity to see and hear their teacher prior to that first day. Some teachers will make phone or video calls during the summer, having an opportunity to talk with the family as well as their future students.

Schools and teachers might look to host class playdates at the school playground allowing students to meet their teacher and classmates in a fun setting. There are many ways to connect with students before the start of the school year, each one helping to establish a climate where students feel safe, welcome, and wanted.

The work continues during the first few weeks of school. During this time, teachers are working to establish a relationship with each student and foster relationships among all students. Establishing a community and team-building activities or icebreakers help students get to know each other's names as well as something unique and special about everyone. Simple activities such as name games (e.g., The Cookie Jar chant, Name Bingo) helps everyone learn each other's names. Teachers may have students bring something in from their homes, such as a family photo, favorite book, toy, or other items to support relationship building.

These activities are opportunities to recognize and celebrate the diversity in the classroom, honoring the differences and similarities among the students. Additionally, this helps to foster the expectation that everyone in the learning community is worthy of being recognized and known.

Class meetings are another way to provide teachers with an opportunity to engage students in important social and emotional learning. Meetings such as these will help positively impact classroom interactions, further supporting the type of environment where students can trust one another and their teacher. Fostering this environment and these relationships helps to link social learning with academic goals, supporting a classroom where students know they belong and are ready to engage with one another.

Teachers need to focus on teaching, learning, cultivating relationships, and establishing a positive environment. One key aspect for teachers to consider is the type of instructional materials that are selected and used in the classroom. Clearly, it is important to use a variety of materials to engage and tap into different students' learning needs. Students can be engaged when manipulatives, movement, or visual art are incorporated into lessons.

Students benefit from having choices as part of their learning experience. This can come in the form of providing a selection of activities during a lesson, independent center opportunities, or choices on how students will be assessed at the end of a lesson. Many teachers offer choices in the types of homework students may complete during the week or month. However, it is essential that teachers make sure that materials are accessible to all students and that they represent the great diversity in the classroom and community. For example, teachers can do this by ensuring children's books represent students in various situations and provide multiple images where students can see themselves reflected in the text.

Teachers must carefully select the types of instructional methods and strategies they will use to engage students with the content to maximize motivation and engagement. Marzano (2017) provides a comprehensive instructional framework that suggests different strategies that can engage learners and help them develop a deeper understanding of different concepts. Additionally, Hattie (2012) has shared research on the types of strategies that have the most impact on student learning.

Teachers will want to research and explore these, adding them to a toolbox of strategies, organizers, applications, and protocols that they can use as part of their daily instruction. Teachers also need to consider how they use time and technology as tools in meaningful ways to support a wide range of students.

Throughout this chapter, you read about two criteria for building engagement and motivation. The first is through fostering relationships. The second is through instructional practices. In the next two scenarios, you will have opportunities to explore both. In the first scenario, you will read a case study of a novice teacher and begin to help the teacher brainstorm different ways of building relationships during the first week of school. The second scenario will have you reimagine different lessons to make them more engaging for learners.

Scenario 1: Don't Smile Until Winter Break

This case study is broken down into three parts, plus one additional part for a final reflection. As you read the case, you will be asked questions. You will be asked what you would do in the specific situation and provide suggestions for a resolution. There is no one right or wrong answer for these questions. The goal is to think critically about what you would do.

Part I: Summer Excitement. Mr. Sonreir just graduated college and was offered his first job as a third grade teacher. He was incredibly excited and spent all summer reading and studying the school's curriculum and texts.

He constructed his classroom code of conduct, list of procedures, and discipline plan.

He was able to get into the classroom over the summer and set up the space. He placed desks to accommodate student groups of four to five to encourage students to work together. There was a classroom library and rug for class meetings. He designed different bulletin boards to have classroom galleries so students could showcase their work. In order to learn more about his students, he started to construct a parent and student survey to give out during the first week of class. He was so excited to start.

Questions

1. What elements of Mr. Sonreir's classroom organization and planning are useful?
2. What suggestions do you have for Mr. Sonreir as he prepares for his new job?
3. If you were in Mr. Sonreir's place, what would you be doing during the summer to prepare? Think of things that might be the same or different from Mr. Sonreir's preparations.

Part II: Don't Smile. The week before school began, Mr. Sonreir met with his mentor teacher, Mrs. Fruncir. She was one of the other third grade teachers. Mr. Sonreir shared all the work he had been doing over the summer and asked Mrs. Fruncir if she had any suggestions regarding a parent and student survey.

Mr. Sonreir was surprised when Mrs. Fruncir responded by saying this incoming class of third graders is very challenging. She felt the parents never came to volunteer, and when they did reach out, it was because they believed their child was being treated unfairly. She also shared that the incoming class has a lot of behavioral problems and some stories of what happened the previous year. She shared that last year, a new teacher in second grade tried to be the students' friend, and the students just walked all over that teacher. The teacher left halfway through the year. It was that bad.

Mrs. Fruncir then gave Mr. Sonreir two pieces of advice. First, do not smile until winter break. Mr. Sonreir had heard of this before but thought that was an old idea and could not believe that teachers still did it. Second, Mrs. Fruncir suggested that he focus on the content and lessons during the first week of school. Additionally, she told Mr. Sonreir not to open the year up with "fun" activities because students will misinterpret school time for fun rather than learning. She suggested that Mr. Sonreir not worry about a survey. She said that a survey is one of those good educational ideas in theory, though it does not work in practice. Furthermore, the information that students and parents provide is not really helpful.

After Mr. Sonreir's meeting with Mrs. Fruncir, he was a little disappointed but decided it was good to hear advice from a practicing teacher. He did not want to get walked on by his students. Consequently, he started to rethink his ideas for the start of school.

Questions

1. What do you think about the advice Mrs. Fruncir gave to Mr. Sonreir? Do you agree with it? Disagree? Why or why not?
2. After hearing this advice from Mrs. Fruncir, what would you suggest Mr. Sonreir do? What would you do? Explain why.
3. A mentor/mentee relationship is important. Think about what you would suggest to Mr. Sonreir. Given his working position and collegial relationship with Mrs. Fruncir, what would be the best approach?

Part III: Back to School Night. Mr. Sonreir had been working at the school for two weeks, and it was now time for back-to-school night. He took the advice of Mrs. Fruncir. He did not send home a parent and student survey. He did not do the fun "getting-to-know-you" games that he originally planned for the start of the year. He spent a lot of time going over his rules and discipline plan. He reviewed procedures multiple times. He avoided sharing any fun stories with the students and kept his conversations with students about content.

The class was very well behaved, but he was not having any fun and did not think the students were really enjoying the year. Wasn't school supposed to be fun?

Mr. Sonreir was happily surprised to see all his students' parents attend the back-to-school night. He shared with the parents what students would be learning throughout the year. He shared with them his code of conduct and discipline plan. At the end of his speech, he asked if there were any questions. Parents raised their hands and asked questions. They asked about where he was from, why he wanted to be a teacher, where he went to school, and other questions that were "getting-to-know you" type of inquiries. He realized he had not shared this information with the parents or the students.

Then some parents started to ask questions about different learning activities. One parent asked if there would be any field trips. Another parent asked if students would get to use different types of technology in the class. A few parents said they would volunteer to help come into the class.

In the end, Mr. Sonreir was really enjoying the conversation with his parents and realized he had a different perspective of them. As they were leaving, one of the parents stayed around to talk. The parent shared that she was concerned because her child said Mr. Sonreir was scary. Her child had a question about what materials to bring into class but did not want to ask Mr. Sonreir because she might get in trouble. As the parent was sharing this information with Mr. Sonreir, he realized he did not even know the student. After back-to-school night, Mr. Sonreir realized he was not letting his students see the real him. He did not really know his students.

Questions

1. What do you think about how Mr. Sonreir handled back-to-school night?
2. What do you suggest Mr. Sonreir should do moving forward with his students in the classroom, with Mrs. Fruncir, and with the parents?
3. Is it too late for Mr. Sonreir to change the culture of his classroom? What suggestions do you have for Mr. Sonreir moving forward? Be specific, and give detailed suggestions.

Part IV: Share and Discuss. After you have read the case study and worked through the questions, it is a good idea to find a colleague, family member, or friend who has either done this activity or ask them to do the activity. Then go back through each part and share your answers to the questions. You might hear different perspectives of what someone might do in this situation. There can be alternative ideas for how to handle these situations. You will also be able to share your ideas and help a colleague understand your interpretation of this case study. Good teachers share stories, ideas, and solutions.

Scenario 2: Spice Up Those Lessons

Students who are engaged in the lesson are less likely to misbehave. It is up to the teacher to create engaging lessons and activities for students. However, it is essential not to compromise the teaching of content just to make a lesson "fun." Content should always drive the lesson as you integrate different creative, fun, hands-on, exploratory practices to hook your students into learning the content.

The following three activities are lessons that could be taught in elementary science, social studies, and math classroom. You must read through the lesson plan ideas and construct a way to modify and spice up the lessons. The aim is to ensure students are still learning the content and are fully engaged and immersed in the learning experience.

Lesson Plan 1: Science

To learn about sink vs. float, the teacher has a bucket of water and ten items (five that float and five that sink). The teacher has the students come to the front of the class and make predictions about whether each item will sink or float. The teacher writes the class predictions on the board. Then the teacher picks one student to test an item. The student goes up, picks an item, and tests it. The rest of the students watch to see if the item sinks or floats. The teacher asks the class what they see and records the result on the board. Then the teacher picks another student.

This is repeated for all ten items. In the end, the teacher asks students if they were right or wrong in their class predictions? Next, the teacher asks if there are similar characteristics of the items that sunk versus floated? Subsequently, students return to their desks and are directed to write about the lab and what they learned in their science journals.

Now, it is your turn to spruce up this lesson. Think about who is doing the work. Whoever is doing the work is typically doing the learning. If the teacher is doing the work, then the teacher is doing some good learning. If one student is doing the work, then that one student is doing some good learning. Your goal as a teacher should be to have all the students doing the work so they are all engaged in the learning process.

Try to rewrite this lesson idea to engage students in the science experiment. You can write it as a full lesson plan, or you can just write a scenario describing what it would look like in your classroom. Alternatively, you can write bullet points of what you would do to teach the science concepts.

Lesson Plan 2: Social Studies

The teacher asks the students to read silently the history chapter about the Constitutional Convention. Once they finish reading the chapter, they are supposed to answer the chapter questions and draw a picture that represents the content of what they read. When they are finished, students can hang up their pictures on the classroom gallery wall.

This is a common scenario. You probably remember reading chapters from textbooks and answering questions. It is not always best practice to read a chapter and answer questions; however, you want to think if it is the best way for students to acquire and retain information fully. Also, will it spark students to want to learn more about the content? Before you begin to reconstruct this social studies lesson, you want to answer the following questions:

1. What content is being covered?
2. What skills are being developed (i.e., reading, writing, etc.)?
3. How are students learning the content with this situation?
4. What type of learners might do well in this type of activity, and what type of learners might struggle with this type of learning situation?

Now that you have thought through the questions, it is your turn to reimagine this lesson. Make sure you are being considerate of the content and skills being developed in this lesson. How does the lesson reflect the diversity of the students' community? Using your own creativity, your goal is to create an alternative lesson that would still meet the content and skills that need to be covered. Proceed in a manner that will engage students and ignite a curiosity to continue learning about the social studies content.

Lesson Plan 3: Math

The teacher gives a math worksheet for adding and subtracting fractions. For each problem, students are asked to begin by drawing a picture to represent the fractions that they are adding or subtracting and then draw a picture of the solution. After students complete the problems, they share their answers with their table group and see the different ways their peers represented the fractions. As students share their work, they are encouraged to correct any mistakes. Once they have shared as a group, the teacher goes over each problem on the board.

In this scenario, the teacher provides opportunities for students to work independently and collaboratively. The teacher also engages visual and spatial learners by having students represent numerical values with pictures.

While this lesson has good aspects, there are always ways to develop it further by adding a little razzle-dazzle. One way to do this is to use a variety of modalities. Could you change the lesson to engage those learners? Or could you change the lesson so that students complete the same work and include a game or scavenger hunt? Another option is adapting it to incorporate tactile and hands-on aspects. Perhaps you could think of multiple ways of engaging students in the content and providing choices in how they demonstrate knowledge?

Based on these questions, you can see there are many ways to revamp this lesson to engage learners, make it relevant, and meet special needs. Your task is to rewrite this scenario that engages learners using different modalities to demonstrate an understanding of adding and subtracting fractions. Describe how you revamped the lesson and why you believe those changes would spark engagement from a variety of learners.

"TEACHER TALK": PRACTICAL STRATEGIES FROM EXPERIENCED TEACHERS

The following three teachers share accounts of ways they engage and motivate students. All three discuss creating experiences in the classroom that build class community and develop relationships between the teacher and students, and also among students. They all have in common the fact that the methods used to build these relationships and promote engagement and motivation are genuine and authentic. They truly care about their students.

Teacher Talk 1

As teachers, it is very important for us to build relationships with our students. I have daily morning meetings to help build relationships with my students. I follow the Responsive Classroom format that consists of a morning message, greeting, activity, and share.

I display the morning message on the board as part of the morning routine. I typically base the theme of my morning message on the National Day for that date (e.g., national read a book day, national pet rock day, etc.). I will often include a riddle, fun fact, meme, quote, or trivia with the morning message. This often leads to discussion among the students, which also helps them build relationships with each other.

Our morning meetings start with a greeting. Not only do I greet the students, but they also greet each other. We mix up the greeting and style of the greeting every day to keep it fun.

The share portion of the meeting allows students to express themselves in different ways.

Sometimes students will answer a prompt orally; other times, students will move to a certain location in the room based on their responses. Partner sharing, polls, and written responses are some other formats of sharing we do. Not only does sharing give me a chance to get to know my students better, but it also allows the students to get to know their classmates. Additionally, I include myself in the share so that students can connect and relate to me as well.

The students' favorite part of the morning meeting is the activity. The options for activities are endless. We do games, brain exercises, creative play, art, and more. It is also a chance to incorporate social-emotional learning. I think it is also important for the teacher to be a part of these activities, as it can motivate students.

Morning meetings may only last about fifteen minutes of the day, but those fifteen minutes are powerful. It enables the whole class to become a community. The connections that are built enable the classroom to run more efficiently as well.

—Teacher Amanda DiPasqua

Teacher Talk 2

I don't care how many education classes you take. I don't care how great you are at solving math problems, writing papers, understanding grammar, teaching how to draw, sing, or use a computer. If you don't spend the time, the necessary time, to build relationships with your students, you will find it extremely hard to be successful in the classroom.

Your class of 24 is almost guaranteed to have varying learning styles, interests, personalities, and most of all, and this is everywhere, very different home lives. Your job as their teacher is to mold this group into their own community—to take this melting pot of students with their questions, their ideas, their thoughts, their problems, their successes—and to make them one.

First, your students need to know that you are a real person, with a real home life, and that you one day sat in the same seat they now sit. It's important for them to know that you have a family, and this helps them realize that you are someone more than just the person standing in front of them. On the first day of school, even before saying good morning, I immediately dive into a story about how my youngest daughter was born in an ambulance in my driveway.

As I embellish this very much true story, I also introduce to them my wife, my oldest daughter, and the fact that I had a previous career before teaching. I mix in a little humor, engage them as the story continues, then end it with: "I'm Mr. Ricci, welcome to fifth grade," as they sit there astonishingly staring. Do I have their attention? Check.

Next, it's important for them to communicate to you how they feel about coming back to school. I use a paper with a bunch of questions ranging from their opinion on the physical classroom, their worries, their expectations, their excitement about fifth grade, and finally questions they have for me.

I spend a good portion of time answering the questions they have for me, and at the same time, I take note of their opinions and expectations for the year. The more they see me as a person, the more engaged they become, and if you as their teacher connect with them on a personal basis—show them similarities in your life that they have in theirs—it does wonders with how you'll reach them throughout the year.

It's very important to build class chemistry. Be sure all of them stand on equal footing—that you value them all the same, even if in different ways. Have them realize that everyone brings something to the table to keep this a cohesive classroom—you have your artists, your writers, your math whizzes, your athletes, your singers, your dancers—the list is endless, and it's important that each and every kid realize they have something to contribute. Find that something in them all, advertise it to all the kids by giving that student their moment, and they'll work for you like you've never seen before.

—*Teacher Patrick Ricci*

Teacher Talk 3

From day one, get to know your students as people. Students like to be part of a group (a community) and feel included. Use phrases like: "Who enjoys . . . Who likes . . . Who is . . ." and have them do something in unison (stomp feet, clap hands, raise a hand/whiteboard, rap on the desk, etc.) to acknowledge their unity. It is the establishment of a community that will assist you with engagement, motivation, and behaviors throughout the year.

Establish those classroom routines early on and be consistent. My students always have the option to call upon a classmate for assistance, always give them an out, and never tell them they are wrong—especially when they are trying. I always reply with, "I like your ideas . . . now, can you call upon another classmate so we can hear what they have to say?"

Try to change the mindset of: "I can't" and "I will not" by reinforcing the phrases "I will try" "I will try even though I do not know how to . . . yet!" If your classroom community establishes a safe environment where students can extend themselves, they will never not try for you, the teacher.

Keep a sense of humor, and do not take yourself too seriously. Remember, students are children—laughter is the best medicine.

Students love to find your mistakes and you can use that: "You will make a great peer editor! I love how you were able to find my error." Your small error will be their greatest victory and boost their confidence. I always tell my students if they learn from a mistake, it is no longer a mistake but a learning experience.

Get to know your student's names DAY ONE!

—*Teacher Bronwyn Lakowski*

IT'S YOUR TURN: CREATE

Throughout this chapter, you have read about the importance of engagement and motivation by building personal relationships with students and creating learning experiences. Now it is your turn to create. In the following three activities, you will recall an inspiring teacher, create an innovative and engaging lesson, and construct "getting-to-know" activities for the beginning of the school year.

Activity 1: Remember Your Teacher

When thinking about engagement and motivation, you might start to think about teachers you had in the past who inspired you. Recalling teachers who had an impact on your journey as a learner and becoming a student is important. For this activity, you will reflect on one of your teachers who inspired you. Create a video (2–5 minutes) of yourself talking about this teacher by answering the following prompts.

1. Who was the teacher? What grade and/or subject did he/she teach?
2. What were the lessons or types of learning activities you remember from this teacher? Why do you think these stood out to you?
3. What were some ways this teacher connected with you as a person? Or ways this teacher got to know you and your classmates?
4. What characteristics do you see in this teacher that you hope to emulate as a teacher?

Activity 2: Whoever Is Doing the Work Is Doing the Learning

When you think about creating an engaging lesson, remember that whoever is doing the work is doing the learning. If the teacher is doing the work of demonstrating, solving problems, reading books, answering questions, and so forth, then the teacher is doing the learning. However, if students are using manipulatives, testing the experiment, solving the problems, reading the story, answering the questions, discussing the book, and researching information, then the students are doing the work and the learning.

When thinking about designing engaging learning experiences, you want to be creative. You might think about having centers, hands-on activities, games, and student experimentation as parts of your lesson. You possibly will think about integrating art, music, or bodily kinesthetic activities to help bring the content to life. Regardless of your fun methods, do not forget that the content and skills needed to drive the lesson. Learning should be fun. However, creating fun lessons does not mean compromising the content and skills that need to be taught.

For this activity, find a lesson you wrote. Keep the standards and student learning objectives because your goal is to re-create a lesson but still focus on the content and skills that need to be covered. Once you have picked the lesson, your challenge is to redesign it in a way that fosters student engagement. Using the list, include two or more of the following methods and instructional strategies in your newly created lesson.

- Art
- Bodily Kinesthetics
- Centers
- Game

- Innovative Technology (create podcasts, videos, etc.)
- Manipulatives
- Music
- Outdoor Adventures (or outdoor experiences)
- Role Play
- Scavenger Hunt
- Student Experiments
- Student Presentations

Activity 3: Getting to Know You

The old adage "Don't smile until December" does not promote the type of positive learning communities we want to establish for our students and teachers. Instead, we want teachers to smile as students walk into a welcoming classroom on the first day of school. We want teachers to get to know students as learners and people. We want students to get to know their teachers and feel comfortable with an adult figure. We want students and teachers to feel confident being themselves in the classroom and build each other's self-esteem.

While these sound like good ideas, it takes work to establish this type of learning community and culture in the classroom. It does not happen by circumstance.

As a teacher, you will want to integrate "getting to know you" activities at the beginning and throughout the year. Your job in this activity is to come up with three activities you would do during the first week of school and one activity you will do throughout the school year.

You will need to do some research for this activity. Begin by interviewing one or two current or former teachers. Ask teachers and discover what are some activities you do during the first week of school to get to know your students. As the teacher describes the activities, ask if they have any resources (worksheets, presentations, lessons, etc.) that they could share with you to go along with the activities. Building your toolbox of resources is important.

Also, ask the teacher what types of ongoing activities they do throughout the school year that build relationships. For example, there are star-of-the-week, mystery readers, gallery bulletin boards, special handshakes, funny hat day, and other endless ways to connect. Again, ask if the teacher has any materials to accompany these ideas that you could borrow.

After you have interviewed one or two teachers and started to collect resources, go online and do a little research. Try to find other creative ways teachers get to know students during the first week of school. Search ways teachers continue to build a classroom community throughout the year. Collect resources and save these ideas.

Once you have talked to teachers and researched online, it is your turn to create ideas that you actually will use. Begin by thinking about the first week of school. Come up with three concrete activities you will do during the first week of school. These activities should help you get to know your students and have students get to know each other. You can borrow ideas that you learned about or construct your own. Make sure you have all the materials you need to implement these three ideas during the first week of school.

Next, you will create one class-building activity that you will implement throughout the school year. Describe the activity and create the materials that will go with the activity. Again, you can borrow ideas and materials you collected through this activity's research portion.

Remember, this activity aims to research ways teachers get to know their students and create a culture of togetherness in the classroom. You want to leave this activity with materials and resources you will begin using during the first week of school. Be creative and have fun with it. If you have fun, the students will have fun getting to know you and each other.

REFERENCES

Danielson, C. (2013). *The framework for teaching evaluation instrument*. The Danielson Group.

Dreikurs, R. (1969). *Dynamics of classroom behavior: Education in-service: twelve, 30-minute Lessons*. University of Nebraska, Great Plains National ITV Library.

Gorski, P. C., & Swalwell, K. (2015). Equity literacy for all. *Educational leadership*, *72*(6), 34–40.

Hattie, J. (2012). *Visible learning for teachers: Maximizing impact on learning*. Routledge.

Jensen, E. (2005). *Teaching with the brain in mind*. ASCD.

Johnson, J. F., Uline, C. L., & Perez, L. G. (2019). *Teaching practices from America's best urban schools: A guide for school and classroom leaders*. Routledge.

Ladson□Billings, G. (1995). But that's just good teaching! The case for culturally relevant pedagogy. *Theory into practice*, *34*(3), 159–165.

Marzano, R. J. (2017). *The new art and science of teaching*. Bloomington, IN: Solution Tree Press.

Maslow, A. H., & Frager, R. (1987). *Motivation and personality*, Third edition. Harper and Row.

Milner IV, H. R., Cunningham, H. B., Delale-O'Connor, L., & Kestenberg, E. G. (2018). *"These kids are out of control": Why we must reimagine "Classroom management" for equity*. Corwin Press.

Postholm, M. B. (2013). Classroom management: what does research tell us? *European Educational Research Journal*, *12*(3), 389–402.

Weinstein, C., Curran, M., & Tomlinson-Clarke, S. (2003). Culturally responsive classroom management: Awareness into action. *Theory into practice*, *42*(4), 269–276.

Weinstein, C. S., Tomlinson-Clarke, S., & Curran, M. (2004). Toward a conception of culturally responsive classroom management. *Journal of teacher education*, *55*(1), 25–38.

Wong, H. K., Wong, R. T., Jondahl, S. F., & Ferguson, O. F. (2018). *The classroom management book*. Mountain View, CA: Harry K. Wong Publications.

Chapter 3

Rules and Discipline

Classrooms are busy social communities that require structure and organization to ensure that all students have the opportunity to engage and learn. These structures need to support a learning community where all students feel a sense of belonging and safety (Dreikurs, 1969; Charles, 2008). To accomplish these goals, teachers need to develop a comprehensive classroom management plan that includes details about rules and guidelines that will support students as they strive to learn social skills that will also help them succeed academically.

An effective classroom management plan should ensure that well-understood rules guide students on how to be important and successful classroom community members (Charney, 2002; Curwin & Mendler, 2008; Malone & Tietjens, 2000; Pinto, 2013). This plan must also outline possible responses to misbehavior that help maintain order in the classroom and ensure that students learn positive social skills to prevent further behavioral challenges (Charney, 2002; Curwin & Mendler, 2008; Kraft, 2010; Pinto, 2013).

Taking the time to identify, teach, and review routines, expectations, and rules helps to create a solid structure that supports student success in the classroom (Canter & Canter, 1976; Glasser, 1992; Kohn, 2006). This chapter will present fundamental information about the importance of establishing rules and discipline in a classroom, along with practical ideas for establishing these in elementary classrooms.

FOUNDATION

Classroom Rules as Critical Frames for a Successful Learning Community

Classrooms need to be effective learning spaces where students can engage in meaningful instruction that helps them to achieve their own personal goals and become positive members of their class communities. This requires that teachers and students identify guidelines that help each function cooperatively and optimally to best support student development.

Kohn (2006) notes that this begins with reflecting on what one needs to be successful within the classroom environment and beyond. Students and teachers both have the right to engage productively in a classroom community. Developing clear and fair classroom rules helps to ensure that students can learn and teachers can teach (Brady, Forton, Porter, & Wood, 2003; Canter & Canter, 1976; Charles, 2008; Charney, 2002; Malone & Tietjens, 2000).

Effective rules provide a framework for positive interactions between classroom community members. Classroom rules cannot possibly include details about every desired behavior and legislate each action in the classroom (Brady et al., 2003; Charney, 2002; Kohn, 2006; Malone & Tietjens, 2000).

Instead, teachers need to work with students to identify a few general rules that help to provide guidelines for life and work in the classroom while making each member of the class community responsible for supporting and following the rules identified as essential (Brady et al., 2003; Charles, 2008; Charney, 2002; Gordon, 1991; Kohn, 2006). Fewer broad rules are easier for everyone to remember and help to promote active thought about what it means to be a positive member of the classroom community (Brady et al., 2003; Kohn, 2006; Malone & Tietjens, 2000).

Classroom rules should represent community members' needs and highlight ways they can be successful at teaching, learning, and interacting. Both students and teachers have expectations for their life and work at school (Brady et al., 2003; Canter & Canter, 1976; Charles, 2008; Charney, 2002). Rules serve as structures that teachers and students can use to help ensure these expectations become a reality (Gootman, 2008). They help both students and teachers make meaning of and comprehend daily life in the classroom by fostering a sense of order and predictability, a climate of respect where children feel safe to take risks, guidelines for behavior, social awareness, and an understanding of the needs of the group as well as individuals (Brady et al., 2003; Malone & Tietjens, 2000). Creating well-developed classroom rules helps ensure everyone can interact positively and productively at school.

There is no one magic set of classroom rules that will support every classroom. Each classroom is made up of unique individuals who have varied needs, expectations, and goals. Therefore, it is crucial that teachers create an opportunity for classroom rules to be developed collaboratively with students, fostering a sense of ownership and responsibility over the class's ability to work and learn together effectively (Brady et al., 2003; Charles, 2008; Charney, 2002; Gordon, 1991; Kohn, 2006).

Ultimately, rules must help to cultivate a caring and cooperative climate of mutual respect (Brady et al., 2003; Nelsen, Lott, & Glenn, 2011; Pinto, 2013).

Additionally, welcoming students into the process of rule creation helps to ensure that the final list is responsive to the needs and culture of the students, allowing for greater student understanding and structures that are representative of students' cultural norms (Pinto, 2013).

Taking time during the first few weeks of school to create, define, and learn classroom rules collaboratively will help to build commitment to the classroom community, minimize classroom disruptions, and focus the precious classroom time on actively engaging in productive learning opportunities (Brady et al., 2003; Charney, 2002; Kohn, 2006; Malone & Tietjens, 2000).

Responses to Misbehavior as Opportunities for Learning and Growth

Taking the time to develop classroom rules with students helps support an effective classroom learning community. However, mistakes are bound to happen, and rules are likely to be broken from time to time (Brady et al., 2003; Charney, 2002; Malone & Tietjens, 2000; Responsive Classroom, 2018). Teachers need to look at misbehavior as opportunities to help students learn to respond or react in more productive ways in the future (Charles, 2008; Charney, 2002; Glasser, 1992; Gordon, 1991; Responsive Classroom, 2018). This requires teachers to develop a mindset of using responses to misbehavior as productive learning opportunities (Charles, 2008; Charney, 2002; Curwin & Mendler, 2008; Gordon, 1991; Milner et al., 2019).

A teacher's learning mindset toward responding to misbehavior shifts the focus from imposing punishments to consequences that help students to recognize the ways their behavior has impacted the community, their personal learning, and possible options for reacting differently in the future (Bear, 2010; Brady et al., 2003; Charney, 2002; Curwin & Mendler, 2008; Milner et al., 2019; Responsive Classroom, 2018).

All behaviors have some consequences. Certain consequences occur naturally as a direct result of engaging in a particular behavior (Brady et al., 2003; Charney, 2002; Gootman, 2008; Responsive Classroom, 2018). For example, if students destroy their work, they will need to start everything over again, or if a student breaks the rules of a game, he/she will most likely not be asked to play anymore. However, not every misbehavior results in a natural consequence.

Teachers need to think about the most effective ways that they can respond to and manage student misbehavior by balancing the needs of the group and the needs of the individual (Bear, 2010; Canter & Canter, 1976; Charles, 2008; Curwin & Mendler, 2008; Malone & Tietjens, 2000; Milner et al., 2019). Ultimately, teachers need to help students develop self-control and understand their behaviors and reactions (Malone & Tietjens, 2000). It is crucial for teachers to maintain a learning mindset toward misbehaviors to ensure that they are promoting a growth opportunity for the student and not simply responding to the student.

Identifying effective and meaningful responses to misbehavior requires that teachers take time to know and understand their students. The goal of effective responses is to stop the misbehavior and work to ensure that it does not occur in the future (Bear, 2010; Brady et al., 2003; Charney, 2002; Responsive Classroom, 2018; Tincani, 2011). Teachers need to understand issues and factors that strongly influence how students behave to best respond to them in ways that will help students learn and grow (Curwin & Mendler, 2008; Charles, 2008; Dreikurs, 1969; Kraft, 2010; Nelsen, Lott, & Glenn, 2011).

Responses to misbehaviors could focus on providing opportunities for restoration, composure, reflection, or imposing some restriction(s) (Gootman, 2008). Additionally, when there is a conflict between students, teachers may foster a dialogue among the children to help bring about understanding and resolution that strengthens the learning community (Brady et al., 2003; Charney, 2002; Milner et al., 2019). It is crucial that teachers take time to work with students to identify possible consequences of breaking a classroom rule or disrupting the community and ensure that they are enforcing any consequences consistently and equitably (Brady et al., 2003; Charney, 2002; Kraft, 2010; Malone & Tietjens, 2000; Milner et al., 2019).

Effective responses to misbehavior engage students in identifying ways they can be more successful in the future. It is important to remember that despite many efforts, misbehavior will occur (Charney, 2002; Curwin & Mendler, 2008; Malone & Tietjens, 2000; Pinto, 2013; Responsive Classroom, 2018). At times, children will experiment with rules and boundaries as part of the normal process of developing their understanding of social expectations (Responsive Classroom, 2018).

Taking time to develop effective classroom rules, set clear limits, build a strong community, and foster meaningful relationships with students will go a long way toward helping to prevent most misbehavior (Bear, 2010; Brady et al., 2003; Charney, 2002; Curwin & Mendler, 2008; Gordon, 1991; Kohn, 2006; Milner et al., 2019). However, it is important to note that teachers do not have the ability to control every behavior that happens in the classroom (Charney, 2002; Pinto, 2010; Responsive Classroom, 2018).

Additionally, teachers must realize that when they do try to be overly controlling, they run the risk of engaging in a power struggle with students, which is not effective or productive in helping to resolve classroom issues (Charles, 2008; Gordon, 1991; Kraft, 2010; Nelsen, Lott, & Glenn, 2011). The goal should always be to respond in ways that will help students learn more effective methods of reacting or behaving in challenging situations.

PUTTING IDEAS INTO PRACTICE

Establishing and Teaching Classroom Rules

One of the first things you want to think about as you set up your classroom is how you will support order and structure that promote student learning. Effective classroom rules are important guidelines that help to advance positive social and academic interactions in your classroom.

Think back to the philosophy of classroom management you created as part of chapter 1. This philosophy will guide you in identifying the types of rules that you think will be crucial to developing an effective classroom learning environment for all students. Be thinking about expectations you have that will support students as they interact with one another, engage in learning activities, move about the classroom, and work to resolve differences.

Each teacher uses a different process to create rules for his/her classroom. Some choose to develop rules that they construct and present to the students, while others collaborate with their students to develop and define the rules for the learning community. In either case, it is more effective to have a few (no more than 5–6) broad rules that guide behavior and interactions in the classroom rather than a laundry list of "dos and don'ts."

Additionally, you want to ensure that your rules are written in the affirmative, explaining what students *should do* rather than what *not* to do. This helps to keep the focus on rules as guidelines for learning key social and emotional skills. For example, rather than a rule like "Do not run in the classroom," consider "Move around the classroom safely." One can see that the first rule identifies one thing not to do in the classroom, whereas phrasing the rule in the affirmative allows for a broader conversation about ways students can move safely about the classroom.

Working with your students to develop classroom rules can be a powerful community-building and learning activity. Taking the time to welcome students into this process gives them a sense of responsibility to the classroom community and builds ownership over their individual behaviors. Start developing the rules with your students during the first few days of school as you establish rapport and relationships and cultivate a classroom community.

Begin by sharing your goals and expectations for the year and then asking students to identify the same. Use these goals and expectations as a frame to talk about ways everyone needs to interact in order to help develop a community where there are positive interactions and a focus on learning. This links nicely to a conversation about the types of rules needed to help make these goals and expectations actualized in the classroom. This helps to establish the accepted "ways of being" for the class.

Once goals and expectations have been shared and communicated, there is an idea about how everyone should interact in the classroom. You can begin to guide your students in developing a set of classroom rules. Using the group's accepted understanding of the "ways of being" in the classroom, start by having students brainstorm rules that will help everyone do their very best to create this type of learning community.

As students share ideas, record all the suggestions, but take the opportunity to guide them to rephrase all suggestions as affirmative statements. If ideas are phrased, "No yelling," ask students to identify what we should be doing instead of yelling. Facilitate this brief discussion to help students identify a way they could rephrase the idea positively (e.g., Use your inside voice). Keep recording students' ideas until all are heard, shared, and discussed.

Use the class's brainstorming of ideas as the basis for creating a few broad rules that will guide interactions and learning in the classroom. You will likely have ten or more very specific ideas on your brainstorming list. Tell the children that it is impossible to create a rule for every single behavior needed to have an effective learning community. Additionally, point out that it is impossible to remember a list of lengthy rules, noting that it would be important to create a few rules that would help everyone be the best they can be.

Guide students to identify and condense similar ideas to form broad phrases that would support the class. As noted earlier, work to develop three to five rules that will help to support the type of community the class has discussed creating. As you go through this process, take time to have students talk about what each rule means and how it will help them create a classroom where everyone interacts positively and has the opportunity to learn. Many teachers also invite students to review and evaluate the effectiveness of class rules midyear. Allowing the flexibility for the students to make suggestions and changes that they believe will best support the learning community.

While there is no perfect way to go about creating your classroom rules, it is important to take the time to make sure that students fully understand the rules that have been established. As part of getting rules set at the start of the school year, take time to teach each rule specifically. Help students envision the enactment of the rules.

As you teach the rules, you want to give students some opportunities to engage in role plays, behavioral practice, and problem-solving activities that will help them deepen their understanding of the rules and what it means to follow the rules properly. You will teach these essential lessons during the first week or two of the school year. For example, you might present students with a scenario related to the rule and talk through ways this was an example or non-example of how to demonstrate following the rule. Role plays help to provide a concrete model for the types of specific behaviors associated with each rule. Additionally, role play allows students to practice the expected behaviors.

Once you have taught each of the lessons, consider having students collaborate on a class book or wall story that names each rule and depicts what that rule would look like and sound like in the classroom. This can serve as a reminder for each rule and be used throughout the school year to review a rule as needed. Ultimately, taking the time to explicitly teach the rules at the start of the school year helps cultivate common classroom behavior expectations and sets up your students for success.

Responding to Misbehavior

Establishing classroom rules and structures to guide classroom interactions should help to minimize major behavioral disruptions throughout the school year. Efforts to create and support these structures help to define desirable school behaviors for the class. However, mistakes, mishaps, and misbehavior are bound to happen even with a teacher's and students' best efforts. When these occur, teachers need to be prepared to respond in ways that will quickly stop any disruptive or problematic behaviors. Optimally, the teacher will help students learn better ways to react and make effective choices in the future. The most effective teachers tend to view their responses to misbehaviors through a learning lens rather than simply punishment.

The ways you respond to discipline issues in your classroom are informed by your philosophy of classroom management. Effective teachers think about the types of support and structures they can provide students to help prevent most types of misbehavior. It is helpful to think about ways you could prevent behaviors like inattentiveness, talking out of turn, disrupting the class, annoying others, lying, or refusing to cooperate. However, it is also important to consider what type of responses you will employ when the behaviors occur.

The way teachers view their classroom and students impacts potential responses. If one approaches his/her classroom from an obedience stance, responses tend to be more punitive. In contrast, if a teacher is looking to cultivate a collective sense of responsibility and community within the classroom, response options will focus on helping students learn from their actions to make more responsible choices in the future.

Managing a student's behavior in the classroom is complex work. It requires that we leverage what we know about our students, find ways to ensure that responses maintain a student's dignity, ensure the behavior stops, and help the student identify ways to prevent the behavior from happening in the future.

In many instances, what may work to stop a behavior for one student may not work with another. Each student has different needs and motivations for behaviors. This can make processing responses challenging for teachers. Additionally, teachers must consider ways to look out for other students' needs, minimize any major classroom disruptions, maintain the classroom climate, and ensure that student relationships can be maintained.

As teachers respond to students' behaviors, it is important to be aware of the different reasons students may behave the ways they do in the classroom. Tate (2007) identifies four categories of behavior: a desire for attention, a desire for power or control, boredom, or feelings of inadequacy. Taking time to get to know students and their needs better helps teachers to try to determine what may be driving behaviors or reactions we are noticing in the classroom.

Identifying the possible motivation for the behavior helps teachers to determine responses that will best support the needs of the individual and class. For example, if a student is exhibiting attention-seeking behavior, a teacher might use nonverbal cues such as proximity and or tapping the student's desk to try to redirect the behavior. Additionally, using positive reinforcement when the teacher finds that student exhibiting desired school behaviors: the teacher can praise the student for positive behavior. Remember that while the first goal is to stop the misbehavior, the ultimate goal is to help the student learn more effective ways of reacting or working to meet a particular need.

Teachers' responses and reactions in the classroom can also drive and impact student behaviors. It is crucial for teachers to be aware of their reactions to misbehavior. Students are keenly tuned in to a teacher's reactions. Teachers' responses can promote positive or negative dynamics in their student relationships. Individuals need to reflect on their initial feelings and reactions to misbehavior when it occurs. While it is natural to be a bit stressed or have a "fight or flight" feeling, teachers must monitor how these feelings cause them to react and behave. Anger, yelling, and finger pointing will not be productive responses.

When responding to misbehavior, calmness represents strength, and helps teachers best process the situation, mind their body language, and ensure they are responding in consistent ways that maintain the goals of the learning community. Additionally, teachers must be keenly aware of their responses to students in their classrooms. As noted in chapter 2, biases and beliefs about students or student groups impact how teachers view and treat students. Identifying and addressing these is crucial to help teachers effectively respond to classroom disruptions and misbehavior.

There are different types of responses teachers can use when responding to misbehavior. Teachers can often mitigate challenging behaviors through low-key responses such as eye contact, nonverbal cues, proximity, setting clear directions and expectations for a lesson, or using a group gathering or focus signal (e.g., a call and response chant or repeating a clapping signal).

More direct responses include holding a short private conference with the student, inviting a student to take a time out or break from an activity, or a student losing a privilege related to the misbehavior. Remember that some natural consequences may occur because of a student's misbehavior. For example, if a student gets frustrated and rips up his/her work or activity, a consequence can be that the student may not be able to participate in what the class is doing at that time. The teacher might also invite this student to take a break until he/she is ready to participate, causing the student to need to complete their work at a time when the rest of the class may be doing something else.

Teachers may also consider making possible consequences clear at the start of the school year. These should relate to the rules that have been established for the classroom, noting the consequence of not following a rule. This helps inform students how electing to break a rule will impact them and helps teachers react consistently to similar misbehavior. Furthermore, it reminds the students that their behaviors have consequences and following the rules is an important responsibility to the community.

Many teachers who collaborate with their students to develop the classroom rules also invite students to identify potential consequences for breaking them. Realize that this requires instruction and guidance. The consequences help to get students to reflect on and learn from their behaviors, not simply punish students. When teaching students about consequences, it is important to note that while mistakes will happen, everyone should strive not to repeat undesirable behaviors again.

Language plays a key role in how teachers respond to misbehavior in the classroom. Denton (2015) identified three types of effective teacher language that can assist teachers with handling misbehavior: reinforcing, reminding, and redirecting language. Teachers use reinforcing language to highlight proper and expected school behavior (e.g., I noticed how many people were using a quiet hand signal to show they had something important to add to the discussion).

Reminding language is a more direct way of pointing out the behavior that is expected at that time in the classroom. This is an effective tool to use as part of the directions in which a teacher will give for a lesson activity or work time. Reminding language can also be used while students are working and the teacher notices misbehavior starting to occur. Teachers use redirecting language when misbehavior is happening to tell the student what they are expected to be doing at that time (e.g., Stop. Pay attention to the speaker.). Using more effective language can help to mitigate misbehavior and get students back on track.

The ways teachers respond to misbehavior impact the classroom community. Teachers must ensure that students fully understand that there will be some consequences if they break classroom rules and misbehave. More importantly, students need to understand that these consequences result from disrupting the classroom community and class learning in some way. Effective teachers can use good structures and low-key responses to remind students of expectations and mitigate many behaviors.

If these types of measures fail to prevent or stop a behavior, teachers can use more direct responses to students. Either way, teachers need to ensure they monitor their reactions to misbehaviors, helping to maintain a calm, firm, and positive presence in the classroom. Additionally, teachers need to ensure that the decisions they make in response to misbehavior stop the undesired behavior, help to maintain the dignity of all students in the classroom, and diminish any disruption to learning.

Teachers make these decisions very quickly. Therefore, it is helpful to think through ideas and possible reactions to possible misbehaviors prior to anything happening in the classroom.

Considering the rules or classroom code of conduct that one will establish is essential, and then considering the disciplinary plan that will allow teachers and students to hold each other accountable is foundational for classroom management. Along with this, teachers need to recognize that students are individuals, and it is important to understand the misbehavior. That does not mean a student is not held accountable for their actions, or that the teacher does not follow the disciplinary plan. Instead, it means the teacher recognizes a need to stop the behavior and reduce the problem from continuing, repeating, or escalating while also understanding that the root cause must be addressed.

The following two scenarios are designed to help you think about rules, disciplinary plans, and responses to misbehavior. Read each case and apply the information you read earlier in this chapter. Your own experiences can help you to answer the questions.

Scenario 1: Mr. Kay's Classroom

The following is a case study of Mr. Kay's classroom. Read the case and identify the procedures, rules, disciplinary actions, and misbehaviors taking place in the case.

Mr. Kay has a list of classroom jobs. During the first week of school, he goes over each class job and models what it should look like. Every Monday morning, he rotates the jobs. He makes sure everyone gets a chance to do each job.

One of the jobs is distributing papers. Mackenzie was assigned the task at the beginning of the week and did a great job Monday and Tuesday. However, on Wednesday, Mackenzie came to school late. When a student is late or absent, the line leader for the week takes over the job until the student returns. When Mackenzie came to class late, she saw the other student was doing her job. She seemed a little upset, but Mr. Kay reminded her that this is the procedure for when someone is late or absent and that she will start doing this job again next time. Mackenzie did not say anything. She just crossed her arms, clenched her teeth, and sat in her seat. Mr. Kay decided just to give her space. He felt she would be fine.

Later in the day, it was time to pass back papers from a previous homework assignment. Mr. Kay gave the stack of papers to Mackenzie to hand out. Mackenzie looked down at the first paper, crumpled it up into a ball, called out the student's name, and threw it to the student yelling "catch" as the paper was flying through the air. Mackenzie did it again and again. Her peers were getting excited, raising their arms, jumping around, and hollering for Mackenzie to throw it to them.

This all happened very quickly and got out of control very fast. Mr. Kay took the rest of the stack of student papers away from Mackenzie and told her it was inappropriate. Mackenzie told Mr. Kay she was doing the job of handing out papers. She added that she was not told how to distribute papers. Mackenzie thought that this was a lot more fun. The class laughed after her response and started heckling, saying, "She's got a point." It felt disrespectful.

Mr. Kay raised his voice and said, "That is enough!" He told Mackenzie that she lost her class job for the rest of the day, and if she did not pull it together, she would not be allowed to do the job for the rest of the week. At that point, Mackenzie ran out of the classroom crying. The class got very quiet.

After reading the case study, try to apply your understanding of the information you read earlier in the chapter and your own experiences to help you answer the following questions:

1. What rules do you think Makenzie broke? Why do you think that rule is important for the class community?
2. What disciplinary action did Mr. Kay take? Do you think it was appropriate? Why or why not? What disciplinary steps would you suggest?
3. What did you notice about Mackenzie's behaviors throughout the day? How did Mr. Kay respond to those different behaviors? Do you have any suggestions?
4. What did you notice about the classroom behaviors or classroom norms?
5. Thinking about your response to these questions, what recommendations would you have for Mr. Kay moving forward?

Scenario 2: Ms. Santos

Ms. Santos was a firm believer in kindness and building a friendly classroom environment. During her interview, the principal asked about her philosophy, and Ms. Santos talked about how she valued collaboration, respect, and inclusiveness. She described these three ideas as the pillars for creating her classroom community.

Ms. Santos got hired for the position. In anticipation of the school beginning, Ms. Santos created a poster with those three pillars. During the first week of school, she described what each of those ideas meant to her, and reaffirmed those ideas into the students. She even had them recite back the three pillars and what they meant. During back-to-school night she communicated the ideas to the parents.

As the weeks progressed, Ms. Santos started to create sayings for the class. If you walked by her classroom, you might hear Ms. Santos say, "If we don't collaborate, we might evaporate," or other catchy phrases. Ms. Santos constantly referred back to the three pillars.

Students in her class started to make side comments under their breath about the pillars. Sometimes on the playground students would be caught mimicking Ms. Santos and making fun of the three pillars.

During a class activity, Ms. Santos had students working in teams. Before they started working, Ms. Santos reminded the class that they would be collaborating and discussed the meaning of collaboration. Shortly after the groups started working, Ms. Santos noticed one group was fighting. The students were fighting over their roles in the group. Ms. Santos quickly walked over and told the group that they were not collaborating. She then asked them to tell her what collaboration means in their class. Each person in the group recited the class definition of collaboration.

Ms. Santos then walked away, and the fighting in that group started again. She quickly returned to the group and said, "I don't understand the problem. Why are you not collaborating the way we discussed as a class?" One of the students responded, "Because that is your idea not ours." The other students in the group chimed in and confirmed this student's feelings. Other groups stopped working and just stared.

Ms. Santos was stumped to hear that response and the ensuing support from other students. She felt it was incredibly disrespectful. She felt she had to handle this situation immediately, otherwise other students in the class might think it is okay to talk to her this way. She was concerned that the students were disrespecting the pillars that she worked so hard to construct. In response, she said all of the students in the group would stay in for recess with her. Ms. Santos told the student who talked back to go immediately to the principal. She told the other students in the group that they would no longer be doing the group activity, and instead read silently.

Now it was recess time, and the students from the group were in her room. As a punishment she had them write the three pillars, what each one meant, and how their actions did not display the expectation of those pillars. Once they finished writing they had to put their head on the desk until recess was over.

After school, Ms. Santos read the papers. The students all wrote the three pillars and the class descriptions. However, none of them were able to accurately describe how their actions were in contradiction to those three pillars. The principal came in to talk to Ms. Santos to ask what happened. When she shared the story and the papers with the principal, she was shocked to hear the principal's response.

The principal said, "It sounds like you are imposing your ideas onto the students. You might believe in collaboration, respect, and inclusiveness but it doesn't sound like you included your students when thinking about what these mean or how students would hold themselves and each other accountable. While these words sound good, it is up to you to work with your students for the words to take meaning."

After reading the case study, apply your understanding of the information you read earlier in the chapter and your own experiences to help you answer the following questions:

1. What assumptions did Ms. Santos make about her students, her classroom community, and herself?
2. How did Ms. Santos discipline the students? Was her disciplinary approach aligned to her philosophy for creating a learning community, or was there some contradiction? Explain.
3. If you were Ms. Santos, and in this current predicament, what would you be doing the next day in school? Explain what you would do and why.
4. Learning from Ms. Santos experience, what ideas might you borrow and use from Ms. Santos? And what might you do differently?

"TEACHER TALK": PRACTICAL STRATEGIES FROM EXPERIENCED TEACHERS

The structures and community teachers build with their students go a long way to establishing the expectations for behavior as well as identifying what will happen when misbehavior occurs. The time spent early on establishing and practicing rules and expectations can help to mitigate many issues that might cause disruptions in the classroom. The following teacher gives some suggestions on ways to establish and reinforce rules and expectations throughout the school year.

Teacher Talk

Discipline has so much to do with the sense of community that you have established. I would love to say that all students will always follow your rules and routines, but that is not life. You will find that students act out for various reasons. All I can say is to be consistent with the rules that your classroom has established and have a quiet conversation with the disruptive student. Most of my discipline issues stem from issues happening outside of my classroom and students not feeling like they are a part of something. Remember, students have a hard time being heard and if you have established a safe classroom, students will not feel they have to act out to be heard.

Keep yourself and your room organized. Have routines established early. Students will function much better with routines in place. I like to color code and/or give a number to everything, for instance, blue means Language Art, number #1 items belong to Elizabeth, and so on.

Do not forget that it is okay to get messy, just make sure everyone knows where the paper towels and soap are kept.

Rules are established after we discuss what we want our classroom to be like and we have already made our own goals for the school year, teachers included. We discuss what would help students achieve these goals and list various ideas. As a facilitator, use questions that make students think: "How should our classroom sound . . . What are students doing . . . Why is it important for . . . Can you visualize what a working classroom looks like, what do you see?"

Students then offer suggestions for rules and all are displayed (I use Post-its). The whole class will then sort the suggestions into topics (Rules for self; classroom; school; greater community). This is usually something that we work on for a few days and it is a wonderful time to offer some guidance. The teacher should point out students doing the behaviors that support their suggestions, such as, "I see that Elizabeth is working quietly and notice how focused she is on her work." Have the class select a number of suggestions that work for their idea of a working classroom. Do not forget as a teacher you have the ability to guide the students to what works.

—Teacher Bronwyn Lakowski

Rules and Discipline

IT'S YOUR TURN: CREATE

This chapter focused on the importance of establishing a discipline plan for a classroom. This plan is a proactive measure to help teachers teach students how to behave appropriately and build ways to react effectively when misbehavior occurs. A classroom discipline plan identifies ways that the teacher will create an effective learning community by establishing a specific code of conduct or set of rules. Hopefully, through the chapter, readers have started to think about what they would create for their own classroom, as well as how they would like to deal with any behavioral challenges they experience.

Now it is time to build your rules and discipline toolbox. In this activity section, readers will work to build a discipline plan and code of conduct they think will be effective. Follow the different prompts to create your tools. Keep in mind these will change and constantly evolve as readers gain experience, and work to meet the individual nature of the classroom and school community each year.

Activity 1: Observation and Reflection—Behaviors, Responses, and Effect

While spending time in a classroom use the chart from table 3.1 Record different student behaviors you observe. For each behavior you record, note how the teacher responded to the behavior. Try to be as specific as possible for both descriptions. Then note the effect the response had on the student, teacher, and the class. After recording your observations, take some time to reflect on each behavior you witnessed. Complete the final column of the chart by noting why you think the behavior occurred and if the teacher's response led to the effect you observed.

Share your chart with other colleagues who have completed this activity. Share your observations and hold a discussion about ways teachers can effectively handle misbehavior in the classroom. Use the questions in table 3.1 to guide your discussion:

Table 3.1. Teacher Observation

Observed Behavior	Teacher's Response	Effect/Aftermath (student, teacher, and/or of the whole class)	Why Do You Think This Happened?

- How did the behaviors and responses impact the classroom?
- How do you think the teacher was reacting to any misbehaviors? Were there mostly emotional and immediate responses or measured and thoughtful responses?
- How did the responses you observed help the student who was misbehaving to learn from the situation?
- How would you have reacted differently to some of the behaviors you observed?

Activity 2: Your Discipline Plan

It is crucial for teachers to think through the ways they will work to create community and discipline plan in their classrooms before the start of the school year. This helps to build a framework that will guide the ways they manage the classroom, help students learn key social skills and assist them when dealing with any misbehavior. For this activity, readers should take some time to develop a classroom discipline plan they could use in their own classroom. Use the following prompts to guide the work:

- Reflect on the philosophy of classroom management created after reading chapter 1. Identify key goals for the classroom discipline plan suggested by this philosophy.
- Identify some ways to develop and support the community in connection to this model. Consider ways that this plan addresses students' varied social and emotional needs. How will your classroom represent culturally responsive practices?
- Identify a set of model rules that will help to support this community. Use these as a guide when working with students to create rules at the start of the school year. How will these support your goals for the classroom?
- Identify some possible types of misbehavior that students may exhibit in the classroom. How might students break the rules? Remember that it is impossible to identify all types of misbehavior, however it is best to try and prepare for common possibilities.
- Review the list of misbehavior and identify effective responses and consequences for each that stops the misbehavior, maintains student dignity, allows learning to continue, helps to teach the student how to make better choices in the future.
- Consider how to teach students about consequences and how they help support an effective classroom community and teach about ways to behave appropriately.

- Identify ways to evaluate the effectiveness of the classroom discipline plan. What would make this a successful plan? What happens if the plan is not working? How can students help to evaluate the classroom discipline plan?
- Identify how you will share the discipline plan with students and families.

Create Activity 3: Creating Collaborative Class Rules

Classroom rules help to establish a frame for appropriate behavior in the classroom. This frame establishes a plan for a successful learning community, where all students can engage and learn safely and comfortably. Involving students in the rule-creation process is a powerful way to cultivate a sense of community and responsibility among the class. This requires a solid plan for guiding students through the rule creation process. For this activity, readers will create a plan that they could use with elementary students at the start of the year to develop the classroom rules and ensure that the students understand them.

- Create a lesson plan to guide students to identify their goals for the school year. Identify how these goals can help them all to be successful in school.
- Develop a lesson plan that will guide students to create a set of rules that will help all students achieve their stated goals. Identify ways to ensure that all ideas are honored. Identify how to teach students to condense a long list of rules into a set of three to five broad rules that would help guide classroom behavior. Identify how to help students phrase the rules in the affirmative.
- Develop a lesson plan for teaching students what each of the rules means. Identify ways to engage students to understand and identify what each rule should look like and sound like in the classroom.

REFERENCES

Bear, G. G. (2010). *School discipline and self-discipline: A practical guide to promoting prosocial student behavior*. Guilford Press.

Brady, K., Forton, M. B., Porter, D., & Wood, C. (2003). *Rules in school*. Strategies for Teachers Series. Northeast Foundation for Children, Greenfield, MA.

Canter, L. with Canter, M. (1976). *Assertive discipline: A take-charge approach for today's educator*. Santa Monica, CA: Canter and Associates.

Charles, C. (2008). *Building classroom discipline*, ninth ed. Boston: Allyn & Bacon.

Charney, R. (2002). *Teaching children to care: Classroom management for ethical and academic growth, K–8*. Center for Responsive Schools, Inc.

Curwin, R. L., & Mendler, A. N. (2008). *Discipline with dignity*, third edition. ASCD, Alexandria, VA.

Denton, P. (2015). *The power of our words: Teacher language that helps children learn*. Center for Responsive Schools, Inc.

Dreikurs, R. (1969). *Dynamics of classroom behavior: Education in-service: Twelve, 30-minute lessons*. University of Nebraska, Great Plains National ITV Library.

Glasser, W. (1992). *The quality school: Managing students without coercion*, second, expanded edition. New York: HarperPerennial.

Gootman, M. E. (2008). *The caring teacher's guide to discipline: Helping students learn self-control, responsibility, and respect, K–6*. Corwin Press.

Gordon, T. (1991). *Discipline that works: Promoting self-discipline in children*. Penguin.

Kohn, A. (2006). *Beyond discipline: From compliance to community*. ASCD.

Kraft, M. A. (2010). From ringmaster to conductor: 10 simple techniques can turn an unruly class into a productive one. *Phi Delta Kappan, 91*(7), 44–47.

Malone, B. G., & Tietjens, C. L. (2000). Re-examination of classroom rules: The need for clarity and specified behavior. *Special Services in the Schools, 16*(1–2), 159–170.

Milner IV, H. R., Cunningham, H. B., Delale-O'Connor, L., & Kestenberg, E. G. (2019). *"These kids are out of control": Why we must reimagine "classroom management" for equity*. Corwin Press.

Nelsen, J., Lott, L., & Glenn, H. S. (2011). *Positive discipline in the classroom: Developing mutual respect, cooperation, and responsibility in your classroom*, rev. third edition. Harmony.

Pinto, L. E. (2013). *From discipline to culturally responsive engagement: 45 classroom management strategies*. Corwin Press.

Responsive Classroom. (2018). *Teaching self-discipline: The Responsive Classroom guide to helping students dream, behave, and achieve in elementary school*. Center for Responsive Schools, Inc.

Tate, M. L. (2007). *Shouting won't grow dendrites: 20 techniques for managing a brain-compatible classroom*. Corwin Press.

Tincani, M. J. (2011). *Preventing challenging behavior in your classroom: Positive behavior support and effective classroom management*. Waco, TX: Prufrock Press Inc.

Chapter 4

Procedures

Students need and want order and structure in their lives, rules help to frame expectations for student behavior, which helps to support a positive classroom climate. However, students also need to learn ways to navigate their day-to-day learning lives within the classroom (Bohn, Roehrig, & Pressley, 2004; Miller, 2008; Responsive Classroom, 2018).

Effective educators plan for and establish classroom procedures and routines that help students navigate all aspects of their life in the classroom, from how to care for personal needs to how to get materials necessary to participate in a math lesson (Bohn et al., 2004; Rawlings Lester, Allanson, & Notar, 2017; Responsive Classroom, 2018). These procedures give students a sense of security and order allowing them to be more independent in the classroom as they engage in learning activities (Bohn et al., 2004; Rawlings et al., 2017; Responsive Classroom, 2018; Tincani, 2011). This chapter helps to frame an effective process that teachers can use to establish effective procedures in their classrooms.

FOUNDATION

All people need to have order and structure in their lives. Classroom procedures help students know exactly how to do the things necessary to actively engage in the classroom environment (Bohn et al., 2004; Brophy, 1983; Jones, Jones, & Jones, 2007; Rawlings et al., 2017).

Well-established procedures help to cultivate a sense of safety, predictability, and security for everyone in the classroom, while also providing students with a sense of agency for assisting in making the classroom an effective place to learn (Bohn et al., 2004; Rawlings et al., 2017; Responsive Classroom, 2018; Tincani, 2011). Additionally, effective procedures also serve to reinforce each class member's responsibility in helping to support a positive and successful classroom community (Bohn et al., 2004; Rawlings et al., 2017; Responsive Classroom, 2018).

Effective classrooms do not just happen by accident; the teachers who lead these classes take a good deal of time planning for their success. Teachers take the time to think through the different procedures and routines that will help them to maintain classroom order and maximize students' learning opportunities (Miller, 2008; Rawlings et al., 2017; Responsive Classroom, 2018). Even before the school year starts, teachers need to think about their learning goals for students and identify key procedures that will help students to self-regulate and focus on actively participating in lessons (Blumenfeld & Meece, 1985; Brophy, 1983; Tincani, 2011). Well-established classroom procedures can help teachers and students make efficient use of time, minimize behavioral challenges, and maximize learning opportunities.

Teachers need to think critically about their classroom layout and learning goals as they determine the procedures that will assist them in helping to maximize student learning opportunities. Procedures are needed to guide students in navigating the classroom (e.g., lining up, getting learning materials), taking care of personal needs (e.g., using the bathroom, putting belongings away), completing managerial tasks (e.g., putting homework away, ordering lunch), and participating in learning activities (e.g., participating in cooperative learning structures, engaging in classroom discussions).

Effective teachers think through the needs in each of these areas and identify procedures that they feel will help students be successful (Brophy, 1983; Miller, 2008; Rawlings et al., 2017). Additionally, it is crucial that teachers take time to reflect on the effectiveness of classroom procedures to ensure that they are meeting the needs of the students, being open to making any adjustments necessary (Rawlings et al., 2017).

As the school year begins, teachers need to review their procedures and identify the few that are critical for students to learn during the first few days and weeks of school (Brophy, 1983). This helps to set an orderly and positive tone for the school year (Rawlings et al., 2017). Effective teachers will identify a plan of when to introduce specific procedures and materials to students to help them be successful in the learning environment (Miller, 2008; Responsive Classroom, 2018).

Identifying the routines is not enough; teachers need to teach students how to complete each procedure and why they are important to learn and do (Brophy, 1983; Miller, 2008; Rawlings et al., 2017; Responsive Classroom, 2018). When teaching a procedure, effective teachers establish their expectations for a procedure, break down the procedure into manageable parts, and explicitly teaching students each part to ensure student success (Jones et al., 2007; Rawlings et al., 2017; Responsive Classroom, 2018). However, it is critical to give students opportunities to practice procedures and receive feedback on their performance (Responsive Classroom, 2018).

As early classroom procedures become well-known habits, teachers can then introduce other materials and procedures students will use throughout the year. It is important to remember to take time to teach the structures for certain teaching strategies (e.g., inside outside circle, think pair share) and give students opportunities to practice them successfully before simply employing a strategy as part of a lesson. As students develop a knowledge of different structures, these too will become habits when used in the classroom. This helps to minimize the information processing students will need to do during lessons, allowing them to focus on using the procedures as tools to support their learning (Bohn et al., 2004; Blumenfeld & Meece, 1985).

Ultimately efficient procedures help to mitigate many classroom management challenges. Effective procedures help to give students a sense of responsibility and provides them with the predictable structures needed to self-regulate in the classroom (Bohn et al., 2004; Brophy, 1983; Jones et al., 2007; Rawlings et al., 2017; Responsive Classroom, 2018). Predictability and well-established expectations help to minimize confusion and down time during lessons, thus limiting opportunities for misbehavior (Brophy, 1983; Rawlings et al., 2017; Tincani, 2011). Well-established procedures help to ensure that there is a specific sequence to lessons as well as the typical events of the school day (Brophy, 1983; Rawlings et al., 2017; Tincani, 2011).

PUTTING IDEAS INTO PRACTICE

Classroom management has been identified as one of the most challenging aspects for a novice teacher, and specifically establishing and executing classroom procedures. When novice teachers were asked about challenging management issues, many responded saying they just did not know why they needed a procedure to prevent or facilitate predictable situations until they were in the moment of struggling in the classroom. For example, one novice teacher shared that she did not know that she needed a procedure for using the pencil sharpener in class. She realized it when she had students getting up constantly during instructional time to sharpen their pencils causing lines and disruptions. She wished she knew in advance that she needed a procedure to avoid this problem.

Other novice teachers shared that they did not realize how much teaching and repetition went into each procedure. One novice teacher shared how she made the mistake of thinking that if she just told the class that they could execute it on the first try, and that they would remember how to do it for each subsequent time. She learned quickly that it is beneficial when each procedure is broken down, practiced, and reviewed. She also described that after long holiday breaks she sometimes had to go back and reteach some procedures.

Although preservice and novice teachers have observed expert teachers, many of them miss the first few days or weeks of school when teachers establish these procedures. Also, expert teachers have these procedures ingrained and embedded into their lessons and might not communicate why they have a procedure and how they have broken down the procedure.

The following two activities are designed to give you the chance to critically think through the process of teaching procedures. You will also hear from some struggling teachers about challenges occurring in the classroom, and you will give advice on some procedures that the struggling teacher could use that would help reduce the management challenges.

Scenario 1: Identify and Create Step-by-Step Procedures

Expert teachers will have procedures for a multitude of tasks that take place during the school day. Such things like a morning routine, passing out papers, handing in homework, checking out books from the class library, setting up and distributing class materials, sending home communication, sharpening pencils, and much more. Teachers also have procedures for things that are not regular daily occurrences. Events like substitute plans, guest speakers, or students being absent.

Teachers even have contingency plans for when there are hiccups that impact instructional plans. For example, when there is a problem with the technology you planned to use for a lesson. Or when the copy machine is out of order, and you do not have the necessary worksheets to distribute to class. Or when the science materials for a lab are not available. Expert teachers have procedures and plans ready to go for all occasions, and know how and when to communicate the information to students.

Procedures for tasks that students do on a regular basis need to be shared early in the school year. These include morning and dismissal routines, leaving and entering the room, classroom jobs, and so on. When first introducing daily procedures, the teacher should follow these steps:

- Step 1: Introduce the procedure and describe why the procedure is important. If you cannot communicate with students the need for the procedure, then you might want to rethink the need for having the procedure. When possible, ask the students for solutions to a situation that needs to have a procedure instituted. Sometimes getting the students invested make them more responsible and likely to follow it.

- Step 2: Describe and demonstrate the steps for the procedure. The younger the students the fewer steps there should be. The recommendation for elementary students is to keep it between two and five steps. That way students can keep track of it on their hand.
- Step 3: Practice the procedure with the students at least three times. The first time do it with the students. The second time, have them do it on their own. The third time is for them to prove to you how well they can do it. Keep in mind you might need more than three attempts depending on the age and the complexity of the procedure.

Now it is your turn to create steps 1 and 2 for the following three procedures.

Procedure 1: Transitions. The first procedure is coming up with a plan to transition students from their desks to the classroom rug, and then a procedure going from the rug back to their desk. To begin, describe why you think having a procedure for this type of transition is important. Next, do a little research. Talk to expert teachers or even research online some creative transitions teachers have used. Take those ideas and construct your own procedure. Think about what will work with your own style of teaching. Once you have that, construct a poster with step-by-step instructions (3–5 steps) to help communicate your procedure with students. Include a visual to represent each step.

Procedure 2: Collecting & Sending Homework. Collecting and sending homework is one of the ways you will communicate with families, so it is important to think about how you will do this in a way that works for you, and is also simple for your families. To begin, think about your school community, and what you know works well for families and maybe some challenges for families that you might need to consider when developing your procedure. Talk to some expert teachers to see what they have done. Then talk to some families about what has worked for them and suggestions they might have to improve the experience.

Once you have heard some ideas, start to construct your own procedure for how you will collect work and how you will send work home. You might have an in-and-out box in your classroom, use folders, implement a mailbox system, or assign a table group leader to help you. There are all kinds of possibilities, but remember you want to think strategically about what will work for you, your students, and your families so that you get everything that is coming in, and that families get to see the work that is going home. Once you have your idea ready, come up with your step-by-step procedure. This one might have a few parts to it, and that is okay. Make sure it is also something you can share at back-to-school night with families.

Procedure 3: Students Calling Out. Student participation is essential for any good learning community. However, how do you make sure all students are having equal opportunities to participate and share their ideas? Teachers might have multiple procedures for this depending on the situation. For this task you will come with two different approaches. As always, it is a good idea to start by asking teachers what they do and research some creative ideas online. When you are ready, come up with the two procedures you would use to call on students to have them participate in class. Describe the procedures, and the different situations you might use for each procedure. Then come up with your step-by-step approach for both procedures.

Scenario 2: Dear Teacher Guru

In Scenario 1, you took the time to review the procedure a teacher constructed, and made it better by deconstructing how to teach and practice the procedure. Now it is your turn to come up with the needed procedure. The following five letters are written to you, the Teacher Guru. These are written from struggling teachers who are faced with different behavioral challenges happening in their classroom. For each challenge, you will come up with a procedure that will help minimize the problem. For each letter complete the following three prompts:

- Prompt 1: Identify the main problem or concern.
- Prompt 2: Identify a procedure that you believe will help address the concern.
- Prompt 3: Describe why you believe this procedure will directly address the problem.

Once you have read through the five letters and completed the prompts try sharing your answers with a colleague. It could be someone who is also a novice teacher. Or you might share this with an experienced teacher to get their view on these situations. You can also think about sharing these with someone who is not in education, and learn their perspective. Discussing situations, talking through how you would solve these challenging situations, and listening to different points of view of how others might handle the problems will only strengthen your own teacher practice.

Figure 4.1. Teacher Guru Letter 1

Dear Teacher Guru,

My students never seem to be quiet. I constantly tell them to be quiet please, but they do not seem to listen. Sometimes they are working in groups, and I notice they are not doing something right. I try to get their attention, but I don't like to yell. Instead, I just go around to each group and tell them the same thing repeatedly. I don't know what to do. How could I get their attention? How do I avoid repeating my directions? How do I solve this problem? I would appreciate your advice.

Sincerely,
Struggling Teacher

Figure 4.2. Teacher Guru Letter 2

Dear Teacher Guru,

My school has all kinds of technology resources for students and teachers, and I feel a little pressured to use them. I borrowed one of the technology carts for the day to try and use tablets, but it was a disaster. Students were all coming up at the same time to get a tablet. It was a mess, and by accident a few students dropped their tablets on the ground. Luckily the tablets still worked, but it was just chaos.

When it was time to clean up, students were coming up at the same time to put back their tablets. Most of them did not put their tablet back in the right porthole and didn't connect the charging cord. It was at the end of the day so I finally just told the rest of the students to leave their tablet on their desk and I would take care of it. I spent an hour after school rearranging the tablets and making sure everything was back in its right place and charging.

I cannot do that again. I would hate to not use the technology, especially since the school administration really encourages it, but it felt like it was more of a hassle than it was worth. I am not sure we even covered any of the content, I was just focused on the tablets. Do you have any suggestions or advice?

Sincerely,
Struggling Teacher

Figure 4.3. Teacher Guru Letter 3

Dear Teacher Guru,

    I feel overwhelmed. Every day I go home exhausted because of how much I am doing. During class I am running in a thousand directions. For instance, in the morning I am taking attendance, handing out papers, collecting homework, setting up table group materials, collecting student forms, taking lunch orders, and organizing backpacks in the closet. That is just the first 15 minutes of the day. Plus, I have students coming up to me the minute they walk through the door telling me about what they did the night before, or asking questions about what they should be doing. I feel bad. I cannot really respond to the students because I am so busy with all the other stuff, and sometimes I feel like I am being curt with them. I feel like I am all over the place. Do you have any suggestions to help me? I realize that how I start the day lays the foundation for the rest of the day, so you can probably guess how chaotic the rest of the day feels. It is just not going well, and I feel like I am going to burn out quickly. I could use your advice.

Sincerely,
Struggling Teacher

Figure 4.4. Teacher Guru Letter 4

Dear Teacher Guru,

    Yesterday morning I woke up sick, and had to call the school saying I wasn't coming in. The principal asked where my sick lesson plans were. I told him I didn't have them, but that the substitute could just have the kids do independent work for each subject. I emailed him the list of what to give the substitute:

- Reading: Students should free read, and write in their journal about what they read.
- Writing: Students should continue to work on their autobiography.
- Math: Students can work on worksheets from their independent math folder.
- Social Studies: Students can read the next chapter in the book and answer questions.
- Extra Time: Students can get on a tablet and do any of the educational apps.

    When I arrived back at school I had a long note from the substitute about all the problems that arose during the day. Supposedly students finished each subject early, and were bored. This caused some misbehaviors. The substitute tried to ask for student volunteers to help, but then everyone wanted to help and there were issues with that. I just don't understand why it did not go well. My class is usually great. Do you have any suggestions? I don't want something like this to happen again?

Sincerely,
Struggling Teacher

Figure 4.5. Teacher Guru Letter 5

Dear Teacher Guru,

I think I am in a little trouble. My principal came down to my room and asked me how many students were out of my classroom at that moment. I told her that I wasn't sure, I thought there was one in the library and one in the bathroom. She then told me that she knew of those two, but also that there was another student in the library, one at the nurse's office, one at the water fountain and two in the computer room bringing the total to seven students.

After school she stopped me again and said that I should know where all my students are at any time for safety reasons. She also thought that I didn't need to have that many students leave the room at the same time.

I understand her point, but how am I supposed to keep track of who is coming and going? I am in the midst of teaching and I cannot keep track of that. I think it is important to give students responsibility, and that I should trust them. If they need to leave to take care of something, then I want to let them do that. Should a student have to wait to go do something just because another student is out of the room? I am not sure that sounds fair?

I am a little stumped. How do I keep track of all of this and communicate this to students in a way that is fair, and doesn't become a hassle for me? Plus, how do I do it without taking away student responsibility? I appreciate any help or advice you have for me.

Sincerely,
Struggling Teacher

"TEACHER TALK": PRACTICAL STRATEGIES FROM EXPERIENCED TEACHERS

In Scenario 1, you were asked to come up with the step-by-step procedures for three different incidentals that might take place in the classroom. For each of those scenarios, you were asked to talk to expert teachers and look online to learn about different strategies teachers are using in their classroom. There is no reason to reinvent the wheel; asking teachers and getting advice from this is a great place to start when constructing your own procedures. Chances are they have tried a lot of different approaches and have thought through things. The following three teachers are sharing some of their advice about establishing procedures for the classroom.

Teacher Talk 1

There are thousands of things that go on during the school day, and there are many procedures that you may not think of to put in place to make your day go smoothly. One thing I like to do is greet each of my students as they come in the door in the morning. This is also an opportunity to teach appropriate greetings.

There are a ton of neat ways to greet your students, for instance giving them a high five, fist bump, hug, handshake, smile, and much more. You can find a bunch of ideas online, and you can post them on your door. This way your students get to choose what greeting they want. This is a small time in the day where you can connect with each and every one of your students.

Another procedure I put in place for the hallways are tickets, points, or rewards. The hallways are always harder especially for our younger students. There are a lot of expectations in the hallway, and reviewing them before you leave the classroom while they are in line is a great reminder for them. We have specific paper coins we give out as a part of our school-wide behavior system, take a few of those rewards with you on your transitions to encourage great behavior.

The last procedure I started doing during my eleventh year of teaching that will forever be a procedure in my classroom is staggered entries. When your students come back from a transition in the hallway and if everyone enters at the same time there is more room for inappropriate behaviors or not following all of the classroom expectations. Now, I will stand in the doorway and let about five students in at a time. It gives them a few extra seconds to put their things away in their cubbies or desks without the entire classroom barging in at one time.

The last piece of advice I would give a new teacher would be to constantly practice your procedures and that consistency is key. You have to continually practice the expected behaviors that you expect in your classroom. You may think that a few times of reviewing them will help, but the more practice the better. Make sure that you are consistent in your expectations and follow through with them. If you are not consistent, it will lead to a power struggle with your students!

—Teacher Lindsay Sutton

Teacher Talk 2

As a teacher, I always thought seriously about procedures and how they improved the classroom and educational process. I thought of procedures as housekeeping in the classroom, keeping things in order. I made sure that the procedure accomplished three aspects: definition, performance, and engagement, described as follows:

1. In order to avoid misunderstandings, clear and brief directions are paramount.
2. Instructions on how the procedure needs to be accomplished.
3. Procedures are to facilitate student actions, such as movement in the classroom, engaging in learning opportunities, and communication with students/family.

I remember my first few years teaching. I always seemed to be telling the students to do things such as, get your books without banging them on the table, don't sharpen your pencil while I am talking, line up quietly, put your homework in the labeled box, and so on. I felt that I was constantly wrapping procedure rules around instruction.

To make the learning environment less serious and more "user friendly," I created just a few procedures that blanketed over all activities. For example, when students transitioned from subjects or groups, the overall procedure was to move quickly and quietly.

At the beginning of the school year, the students needed to practice the procedures and this took time. However, in the long run, it was a timesaver, because the classroom ran smoothly for the entire year. Sometimes we had to tweak the procedures to accommodate various learning styles.

Students were my best enforcers of procedures. There are always students who are not shy in pointing out when their fellow classmate is not onboard. As long as their guidance is done with respect and kindness, it can initiate a camaraderie among students.

—Teacher Frances Flicker

IT'S YOUR TURN: CREATE

Think back to the introduction chapter in which we talked about the classroom being a ballet. The teacher and students are all engaged in this ballet and there are leaps, jumps, lifts, and turns going on simultaneously. However, for the ballet to run smoothly it must be choreographed and rehearsed. Procedures and routines are the choreography for the classroom. Now that you have thought through the need for different procedures and read from expert teachers about ideas they implement in their own classroom, it is time for you to create. In the following two sections you will construct your own procedures and routines.

Create Morning and End of the Day Routines

How do you want to start each day? This sets the foundation for how the rest of the day will go. Something to think about is making sure every student feels welcomed, and a sense of belonging right when they walk through the door. Each student should know what he or she should be doing, it gives them a sense of responsibility. It also allows you the teacher to be present and in the moment welcoming your students and engaging with them, rather than running around. For this section you will create a "Morning Routines" poster. This poster should include five to ten items, a checklist, and include a visual to go with each item. The last item should be something that engages students in a learning activity that they could do until you are ready to start the school day.

Now that you have thought about the morning routine, it is also important that you consider the end of the day routine. You do not want the bell to ring and then have students in a mad rush trying to put away things and collect their belongings. Instead you want to think about a systematic approach. For this part of the activity, you will create an "End of Day Routines" poster. Just like the other poster, you are going to make a five- to ten-step checklist for students. Students can then look at the checklist and know each day what they need to do as they prepare to leave school. Include a visual to go along with each item of the checklist.

Once you have created both posters, share it with another teacher. Get their advice and see if there is anything they might suggest adding to your morning and end-of-the-day routines.

Create Procedures for the Small Stuff

"Don't sweat the small stuff," just create a procedure for it. Throughout the day teachers will juggle a lot of incidentals including collecting and passing out papers, distributing materials, taking attendance, monitoring hall passes, and more. For this section you will pick three incidentals from the list. For each incident you will create a poster that could be displayed in the classroom that communicates the procedure to students, make sure to include visuals.

After you create the poster, you will then write out the step-by-step procedure. Then include a short paragraph describing why you need this procedure. This is important because you should be able to communicate with your students why this procedure is necessary, and it should connect it back to your rules or code of conduct. Finally describe how you will teach and practice the procedure.

List of Incidentals
- Calling on Students to Share
- Class Jobs
- Classroom Library System
- Daily attendance and lunch count
- Handing in Papers
- Hanging up coats, backpacks, and lunches
- Homework
- Information for Absent Students
- Information for Volunteers
- Lining Up
- Monitor Noise Levels
- Passing out Materials
- Passing out Papers
- Out of Class Procedures (bathroom, nurse, library, etc.)
- Pencil Sharpening
- Students Using Materials during Instruction
- Transitions from Desks to Rug
- Walking in the Halls

REFERENCES

Blumenfeld, P. C., & Meece, J. L. (1985). Life in classrooms revisited. *Theory into Practice, 24*(1), 50–56.

Bohn, C. M., Roehrig, A. D., & Pressley, M. (2004). The first days of school in the classrooms of two more effective and four less effective primary-grades teachers. *The Elementary School Journal, 104*(4), 269–287.

Brophy, J. E. (1983). Classroom organization and management. *The Elementary School Journal, 83*(4), 265–285.

Jones, F. H., Jones, P., & Jones, J. L. T. (2007). *Tools for teaching: Discipline, instruction, motivation.* Fredjones.com.

Miller, D. (2008). *Teaching with intention: Defining beliefs, aligning practice, taking action, K–5.* Stenhouse Publishers.

Rawlings Lester, R., Allanson, P. B., & Notar, C. E. (2017). Routines are the foundation of classroom management. *Education, 137*(4), 398–412.

Responsive Classroom. (2018). *Teaching self-discipline: The Responsive Classroom guide to helping students dream, behave, and achieve in elementary school.* Center for Responsive Schools, Inc.

Tincani, M. J. (2011). *Preventing challenging behavior in your classroom: Positive behavior support and effective classroom management.* Waco, TX: Prufrock Press Inc.

Chapter 5

Designing the Physical Classroom

As teachers strive to create an environment where students can learn and thrive, they must look carefully at the ways that the classroom's physical space is organized and utilized. Effective classroom environments are safe, welcoming spaces, that invite students to explore new ideas and actively engage in learning challenging opportunities (Bucholz & Sheffler, 2009; Clayton, 2001; Gremmen et al., 2016; Miller, 2008; Tate, 2007).

Creating a physical space that supports a positive climate takes planning, effort, and some experimentation in order to meet the varied needs of all students (Brophy, 1983; Clayton, 2001; Miller, 2008). This chapter provides information about the importance of a positive and effective environment, why this is so important to student learning, and ways teachers can create an effective physical classroom space.

FOUNDATION

The physical spaces where students learn can either support or impede their successful learning and development (Bucholz & Sheffler, 2009; Gremmen et al., 2016; Tincani, 2011). The arrangement of furniture as well as placement of and access to materials all impact the ways in which students interact with one another and the learning (Clayton, 2001; Gremmen et al., 2016; Kounin & Sherman, 1979; Rosenfield, Lambert, & Black, 1985; Roskos & Neuman, 2011; Tate, 2007).

It is crucial for teachers to think about their classrooms as spaces that are designed to support students' physical, social, and academic needs, recognizing the need for flexibility, and acknowledging that it is not realistic to expect that one type of arrangement will work for all students (Bucholz & Sheffler, 2009; Good & Power, 1976; Gremmen et al., 2016; Roskos & Neuman, 2011; Tate, 2007; Tincani, 2011). Teachers need to take time to plan for seating options, the ways the walls will enhance the environment as well as where learning materials will be placed and accessed.

When starting to think about designing the physical space of the classroom, teachers must consider the goals, beliefs, and philosophy that drive their instruction (Tate, 2007; Miller, 2008; Rosenfield, Lambert, & Black, 1985; Roskos & Neuman, 2011). It is not realistic to expect that all students will be coming to school ready to stay seated in one place for multiple hours a day, this does not mirror daily expectations outside of school (Tate, 2007). As teachers think about ways they will arrange furniture in the room, they want to ensure that the design will facilitate student interactions as well as provide some options for variety and movement (Bucholz & Sheffler, 2009; Clayton, 2001; Gremmen et al., 2016; Responsive Classroom, 2018; Roskos & Neuman, 2011; Tate, 2007).

It is crucial to remember that a well-organized classroom promotes a sense of safety and security among students (Emmer, Everston, & Anderson, 1980). Teachers need to consider how much space students will need to work and collaborate as well as how students will move about and navigate the classroom as they engage in a variety of learning activities (Brophy, 1983; Good & Power, 1976; Gremmen et al., 2016; Tincani, 2011; Responsive Classroom, 2018). This helps to ensure that students will have easy access to all materials necessary to safely and actively participate in lessons. However, teachers also need to consider how furniture arrangement will allow them to see and observe students as they are working in different spaces to ensure they can support their learning and mitigate any opportunities for misbehavior (Clayton, 2001; Roskos & Neuman, 2011; Tincani, 2011).

Along with thinking about furniture placement, teachers need to think about the ways they will choose to decorate and display items throughout the classroom. Small touches such as having plants and soft pillows around the classroom can help to create a sense of warmth and welcome in the classroom, making the classroom feel more like a home environment (Bucholz & Sheffler, 2009; Clayton, 2001; Miller, 2008; Tate, 2007). The colors of the walls, as well as the decorations, can also help to promote a positive, safe, and welcoming climate within the classroom (Bucholz & Sheffler, 2009; Emmer, Everston, & Anderson, 1980; Responsive Classroom, 2018).

The classroom walls can also function as additional teaching and learning tools (Clayton, 2001; Miller, 2008; Responsive Classroom, 2018; Tate, 2007). Just as with the furniture, teachers must carefully consider where they are placing displays and bulletin boards around the classroom (Clayton, 2001; Miller, 2008; Responsive Classroom, 2018). It is important to consider decorations and displays critically to ensure that items are functional and not overwhelming or distracting to students (Clayton, 2001; Responsive Classroom, 2018; Roskos & Neuman, 2011; Tate, 2007). Teachers want to include a mix of functional displays (e.g., interactive word walls, anchor charts, and schedules) with celebrations of student work (e.g., student writing, student artwork, or displays of student projects). The design of the classroom should ensure that all students can feel welcome as well as have ample opportunities to engage in learning (Bucholz & Sheffler, 2009; Clayton, 2001; Emmer, Everston, & Anderson, 1980; Miller, 2008; Responsive Classroom, 2018; Roskos & Neuman, 2011).

PUTTING IDEAS INTO PRACTICE

Setting up the classroom is one of the first things teachers dream about. However, it is not simple. There are a lot of aspects teachers must consider. Teachers need to address the limitations and possibilities of the types of materials and resources that are accessible. For example, what is the style, shape, and size of the desks? Do you have a classroom library? Are stools or chairs available and are there any creative seating options (i.e., bean bags, rugs)?

There are factors a teacher must consider when laying out the classroom design. The shape and size of the classroom, bulletin boards, windows, and lighting play a significant role in classroom design. For example, what is the most effective way to position desks in relationship to the classroom door, outlets, wall space, chalkboard, or whiteboard? Do students and teachers have convenient access to closets and cubbies? In addition, there are codes to observe, such as fire lanes. Remember that all spaces create a learning area to work.

Then there are logistical considerations a teacher must think about, and these can have implications for classroom management. You want practical things to be accessible without being disruptive. For example, where does the teacher put the trash can? If you put it at the front of the class, do you have students walking pass each other every time someone needs to throw something out? Where do you place the out-of-classroom hall pass? Where do you place the pencil sharpener and tissue box? Little things can make a big difference.

The space also needs to reflect a teacher's philosophy. For instance, if a teacher believes in student accountability and responsibility, then the teacher needs to design a space that supports this by having materials and resources accessible for students to get. Or if a democratic classroom is a key component of his/her philosophy, then possibly having a rug for the class to come together and meet on might be one way to connect the teacher's philosophy to the design of the classroom.

Finally, a teacher must remember to be flexible. Each class will have its own unique character of students and the classroom design will need to adapt and reflect the students. Keeping all of this in mind, the following two activities are designed to help you think critically about different classroom designs, and then think about how the design needs to compliment the needs of students. Adaptability and flexibility are key to successful and continuous classroom design.

Scenario 1: Identifying Pros and Cons of Classroom Space

The classroom design and placement of items around the class tells a lot about the type of teacher and about the type of learning experiences that take place in the classroom. For example, a classroom that has materials hidden away from students, might tell you the teacher wants to have control of those materials and not have students getting materials without assistance. Or a classroom that has all the materials accessible for students might suggest the teacher does not want to be responsible for the materials and instead wants students to be accountable for getting the materials they need. A classroom that has the cubbies right next to the door can indicate a procedure for what students do when they first enter the classroom. The design of the classroom matters in terms of teaching, learning, and classroom procedures.

There is no right or wrong way. If there was, all the classrooms would look the same. However, it is important to think about the benefits and challenges associated with different classroom designs. A teacher must consider his/her own teaching style and the different management procedures he/she wants to establish, and make sure the classroom design aligns.

In this activity you will examine three different classroom layouts. For each classroom you will answer a series of questions. These questions are designed to have you critically think about the design and logistical factors. For each classroom you will also propose benefits and challenges you might foresee in that type of learning space. At the end you will then start to look across the learning spaces and pick out aspects that would work for you, and align to your philosophy and style of teaching.

Classroom 1. In this classroom you will find a lot of different learning spaces. There is the traditional seating section with desks in groups. There are also some alternative seating options for students including a classroom library with beanbag chairs, an open rug, a computer station, and a large circle table for group work that might not be done with their desk groups. The variety might be nice for certain learners, but it might not work for all students. The setup also works for some teaching styles, but not all. There are great features of this classroom space, but there are also some challenges depending on the students and teacher. Take some time examining the space (see figure 5.1) and answering the questions.

Designing the Physical Classroom 63

Figure 5.1. Classroom 1

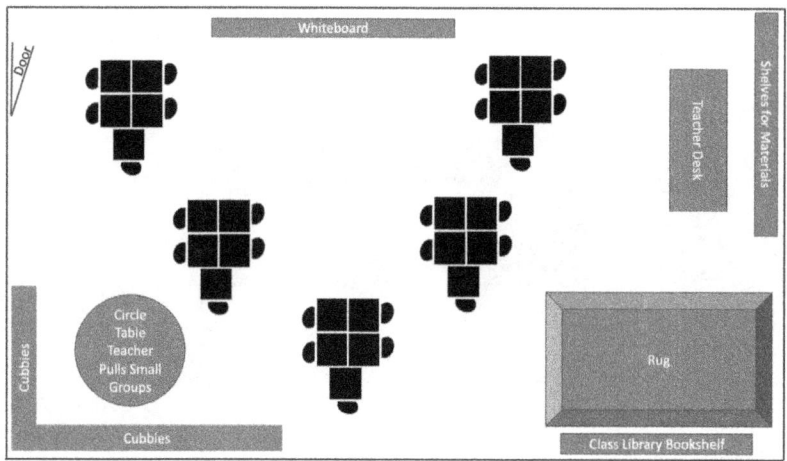

Questions for Classroom 1

- There is no set teacher desk in this classroom. What do you think that tells you about the teacher and the type of teaching happening? Would this work for you? Why or why not?
- What type of learners might do well in this space? What type of learners might struggle in this kind of space? Why?
- Where would you put the trash can(s) and pencil sharpener? What else do you think is missing from this classroom space that you would want to add? Where would you put it?
- What do you like about this classroom? What don't you like about this classroom space?
- Would this work for you? Why or why not?

Classroom 2. This classroom provides table groups but in a U-shape formation. It can give the illusion of each group having a front row seat. It also provides a lot of space in the middle that might be used by the teacher in a variety of ways. This room provides designated space for students to meet at the rug and for small groups to be pulled. In addition, notice how both of those spaces are constructed in the back of the room, behind the desk groups. That probably was intentionally done to reduce distractions.

Pay attention to where the teacher desk is located. Remember there is intentionality in what is in the room and where it is placed. It can tell you a lot about the types of instructional practices, and methods this teacher uses. As you study this classroom setup you will probably identify aspects that you like and work for your own style, but there might be things you would change. Examine the classroom (see figure 5.2) and answer the questions.

64   Chapter 5

Figure 5.2.   Classroom 2

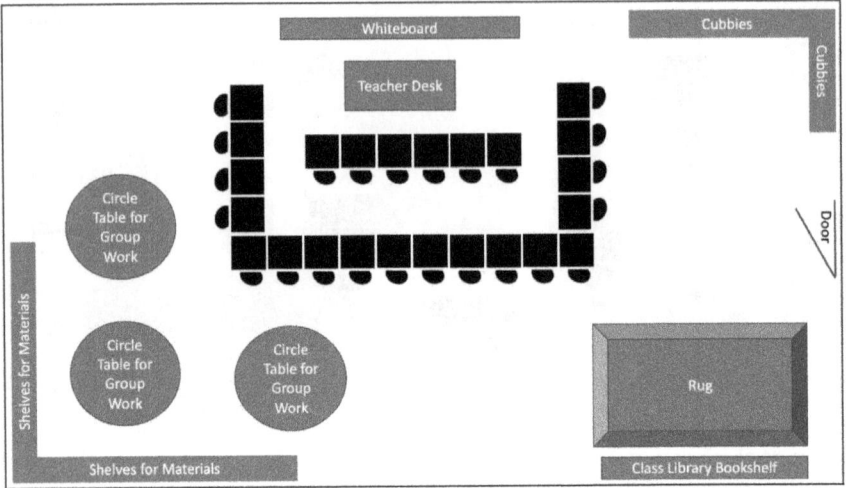

Questions for Classroom 2

- If you were observing this classroom, what type of teaching would you expect to see? Why? What type of teaching would not work in this classroom space? Why?
- What type of learners might do well in this space? What type of learners might struggle in this type of space? Why?
- Notice the classroom door is up front near some of the desks. Do you think this might be a distraction for students? What type of learner might you avoid putting near the classroom door? What type of learner could you put near the door?
- Notice where the cubbies, shelves for class materials and class library are located. Do you find these accessible for students? What would you keep or change about these?
- What do you like about this classroom? What don't you like about this classroom space?
- Would this work for you? Why or why not?

Classroom 3. This classroom is set up to have desks in a U-shape formation, which can be great for class discussions but also supports students' individual work. This room also provides designated space for students to meet at the rug and for small groups to be pulled. The room has three large circle tables for collaborative group work, and a rug that can be used in a variety of ways including independent time, partner work, small groups, or for alternative learning. There is also storage space for students' belongings and classroom materials.

Notice how the shelves for class materials are located behind the teacher desk, which might mean the teacher does not want the students to have access to those materials. There is intentionality in the placement of the teacher desk, student desks, materials, and class library. As you study this classroom setup you will probably identify aspects that you like and work for your own style, but there might be things you would change. Examine the classroom (see figure 5.3) and answer the questions.

Figure 5.3. Classroom 3

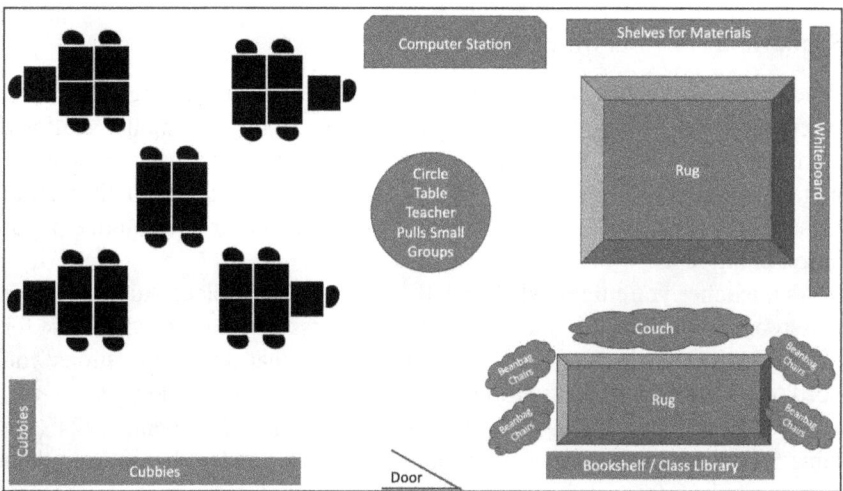

Questions for Classroom 3

- What types of instruction do you imagine seeing in this classroom space? Is that the type of instruction that works for you? Why or why not?
- What type of learners might do well in this space? What type of learners might struggle in this classroom design? Why?
- Notice there is a large empty space in the top right corner of the classroom. What would you suggest adding to that space?
- Notice that the cubbies are right when students enter the classroom. Also notice how the shelves for materials and classroom library are situated in the back of the class near open workspaces. What do you think this says in terms of student responsibility?
- What do you like about this classroom? What don't you like about this classroom space?
- Would this work for you? Why or why not?

Now that you have examined these classrooms, think about what you would like to borrow from each and integrate into your own classroom. Also think about what you did not like, and try to ask yourself why. Sometimes knowing what you do not like is just as important as what you do like. Later on in the chapter you will have the opportunity to create your own classroom design. You will be able to use ideas from this activity to help you think through and construct your learning environment. Moreover, classroom design is an effective tool that can make a difference in instruction and classroom management.

Scenario 2: The Seating Chart

When designing your classroom, you think about how you arrange the desks, where you put different learning spaces (class library, computer stations, community rug, etc.). You contemplate where you place class resources or materials students might need to access throughout the day. Thinking about these things is crucial; however, you also need to consider your unique population of students.

As a teacher you might ask yourself, where will you place students in the classroom? You will think about how your classroom design will work for different types of learners? Maybe you ponder what accommodations you need to offer some students who might be challenged by this design?

For this activity you have been given a class list of students 1–24 (see table 5.1). Each student has a description that was shared with you from their former teacher. After you have done your initial read through of the descriptions, pick a classroom layout from Activity 1 that you think would fit best for this unique class of student. Then you will take that layout and place each student keeping in mind the descriptions provided. Remember you want to consider the needs of individual students and use that to create a positive and collaborative learning environment for the entire classroom community.

As you work through this activity you might be wondering where the answer key is. It is important to remember that there is no right or wrong way to group the students or assign seats. Oftentimes, you might think of putting a group of students together for good reasons, but when you actually have those four or five students together it just does not work. That is okay, you will move them and rearrange students until it does work. You also want to remember that throughout the year you should be moving students.

It is important that students have opportunities to get to work with different people and experience the learning environment from different places in the classroom. As the school year progresses, and as you get to know students and get to know each other, you will move them around the classroom.

Oftentimes novice teachers will ponder the idea of allowing students to get to choose their seat. As you have read before, giving students choice is

Table 5.1. Sample student class descriptions

Student	Description	Student	Description
1	Eager to participate. Hand is always raised to answer questions and be a helper.	13	Has a behavioral IEP.
2	Very social.	14	Very good friends with students 7 and 20. Sometimes a little cliquish.
3	Wears glasses, seems to have trouble seeing far.	15	Great student, right on grade level. Parents will ask at back-to-school to have student sit up front.
4	Gets up a lot to sharpen pencil, throw out trash, get materials, etc. Seems to need opportunities to get up and move.	16	Absent a lot, constantly playing catch up.
5	Has an academic and behavioral IEP. Has a helper who comes in and sits with the student.	17	Works really well with student 9.
6	Wears glasses, trouble seeing the board sometimes.	18	After a mini lesson or directions, the student always has follow-up questions about what to do.
7	Very good friends with students 14 and 20. Sometimes a little cliquish.	19	Great student who wants to help. Good working with others.
8	Advanced for the grade level, but is quiet and might not let you know.	20	Very good friends with students 14 and 7, who are sometimes cliquish, but this student will be social with everyone.
9	Quiet.	21	Trouble sharing and working collaboratively with others. Thinks is always right.
10	Follows directions. Gets concerned and anxious when peers are not following directions, fear of getting in trouble.	22	Great student who wants to help. Good working with others.
11	Works well with others. Great listener.	23	Advanced for the grade level. Is good at helping others.
12	Student is identified ESL.	24	Constantly raising hand to answer questions.

a great way to promote student responsibility and accountability. Choice can also motivate and engage students because they feel a sense of ownership.

While there are benefits associated with giving students choice in selecting their seat, you also need to consider challenges that might arise. For starters, students might not always make the best choice when it comes to where they should sit, and who they should sit with. The other thing to consider is the student who does not know anyone or might not feel they have strong friendships in the class. That students might become very anxious and worried. You want everyone to feel welcomed and a sense of belonging. If you decide to allow students to select their own seat you want to consider the challenges and make sure to find ways to address those.

The goal is to construct a classroom space that is a positive learning environment for all students. If the layout or the seat assignments are not working, it is okay, you can always move things around.

"TEACHER TALK": PRACTICAL STRATEGIES FROM EXPERIENCED TEACHERS

No two classrooms will be the exactly same. Every teacher has a different style of teaching, which in turn means they will have a different approach for designing and decorating their own classroom. Although classroom spaces will look different, it is valuable to hear experienced teachers think about classroom design. The following excerpts are from experienced teachers who have advice about what to think about when designing a classroom.

Teacher Talk 1

I truly believe the classroom environment is an essential aspect of student success and engagement; it is an extension of your educational philosophy and instructional approach. Utilizing the classroom strategically has been very beneficial to my teaching success.

First, let's talk about seating. The seating arrangement in a classroom works best when it reflects the way you design lessons and organize instruction. For example, I implement a lot of cooperative group work and student conversation, so I usually seat my students in table groups. I want to note these groupings are not always even, for example all students in groups of four. Some students may work best in a group of two, some may be better in a group of three, it all depends on my students and even the layout of the room.

In addition, I change my seating arrangements often. I find students like change and benefit from working with different students throughout the year. One thing to note, seating design and student placement is most successful when it reflects the individuals in your class, in this sense it is dynamic and reflects a consideration of personalities, ability levels, and learning styles. So, even though I would usually have table groups, I would change to a circle or U-shape if a unit or plan called for it.

I also believe in the aesthetics of an environment, so I think a lot about how to utilize the physical space so that it flows and is comfortable. I have used lamps in my classrooms to have softer lighting (depending on fire codes), brought in furniture, plants, rugs, and so on. I have even painted walls. What you choose to do with the physical space may be dependent on the school and parameters in which you work, but creating a comfortable and warm space matters, especially at the elementary level. Students will have more investment and engagement if their environment reflects care. Relatedly, keeping your classroom clean, well-organized, and uncluttered is also incredibly important.

Finally, and this is the most crucial piece in my opinion. Your walls and room should "teach" and display a lot of student work. Word walls, anchor charts, and graphic organizers should be posted and students taught to utilize these resources every day during lessons. However, less is more, what hangs should be relevant to lessons and units you are currently teaching. Too much becomes confusing or simply ignored by the students.

Beyond teaching tools, student work should fill your space. I know my students had a different sense of accountability for the assignments they completed knowing I would hang them up for all to see. Not to mention the sense of pride they feel, seeing that what they do is displayed and celebrated. Seeing their work around their classroom also gives students buy-in as well as a reason to put forth their best effort.

Don't underestimate the importance of your classroom design and environment. Utilizing these elements to your advantage inevitably supports the success of your students. Your room really is an extension of who you are as an educator.

—Teacher Dana DeMinico

Teacher Talk 2

One of the biggest buzzwords that I learned three decades ago as a student teacher was that people in this profession had to be "flexible." Lingo has come and gone as education has adjusted with the growing needs of our communities, but "flexible" has held strong. When districts interview new teachers, they are looking for candidates who prove they are flexible. Teachers prove this skill every day with the way they ebb and flow with what each student in their class currently needs.

About fifteen years ago, I started to use the word flexible even more literally, as I started to bring some flexible seating options into my kindergarten classroom. I had just switched from fifth grade to kindergarten, and it was eye opening to me how my little people needed movement breaks and stimulation constantly. Apparently, kids need to be flexible too! I very simply added some yoga mats, a few cute pillows, and some yoga balls and considered myself to have a "flexible seating" classroom. While that really wasn't the case with the way I used it, it was still a first step for me in what I wanted my overall goal to be. I was able to witness the choices students made, how some worked better one way, and some worked better another—and I envisioned what I could create with better resources.

Fast forward to my current third grade position in a different school district. I was given the opportunity to become one of two classes in our building that was officially a flexible seating classroom. Excitement ran through me as I poured through catalogs looking for all the amazing things that I had envisioned for my kindergarten class just a few years before. There were so many choices and I struggled to narrow down to create the very best that I could possibly imagine. The thing is, with flexible seating, there is no one way to make it perfect.

Even with my limited budget in my kindergarten room, I could have made it just as wonderful as what I have now with the resources offered to me. The thing that makes a flexible classroom perfect is having options, choices, and rules.

I currently have twenty-six students in my room, so I have them divided into four groups. Every Monday morning a new group has first choice of their seats for the week, and the other groups follow through until everyone has a seat. Weekly rotations may not work for everyone, but I tried monthly, and I felt like it just didn't give the kids enough flow through the seats. I typically have five main types of seats: something high, something low, something with soft movement, something with firm movement, and something standard.

We have tall tops, we have tables low enough for kids to sit on the floor, we have yoga balls (in chair stands with a back), we have accordion wobble stools, and we have standard desks with standard chairs. Some tabletops are white board, and some are not. Nobody technically "moves in " so they don't keep things at their seats except their name tags and pencil tracks. This makes storage an issue, so I also have 1.5-liter drawers for each student. The drawers are stacked in twos on the closet floor, and it is where they keep everything else that they need.

All students also sign a contract that states they will use the seating appropriately, and the teacher always has the right to move someone if they are not using the seats correctly. It sounds like a lot, but it is extremely organized and allows lots of organized class movement as well as individual, independent movement.

I love the way my class has evolved, and I realize the options are endless no matter what the budget. Any janitor can help you lower a table to floor height. Students can sit on the floor, donated carpet squares, or even low stools, like the ones used for toddlers to reach the bathroom sink. Yoga balls can be economical if you just purchase the ball. You will want to rig a pool noodle to keep it in place if it isn't in a stand with a back.

Yoga mats are a great way to make a space, so clipboards would be necessary for writing. Storage crates or multi-gallon buckets can have cushions made to top them, and often parents will donate items like this if you are financing a classroom like this on your own. Chair pockets can be used to hold the essentials if you don't have the space or the finances available to purchase drawers. It can be done!

Are my kids smarter? Better behaved? More ready for fourth grade? I don't think that any of those things would be 100 percent true all of the time . . . but I can say that my kids love learning, and they invest a lot of themselves into the community that we are building in our classroom. Our flexible seating has a lot to do with that.

—Teacher Kristen Cheney

IT'S YOUR TURN: CREATE

Throughout this chapter, you have experienced a variety of activities. These have included a review of sample classroom setups and connections between classroom design and instruction. While analyzing different classroom designs, you were able to think about the placement of students to meet different learning and behavioral needs. You also heard from practicing teachers and their recommendations for designing and staging classrooms. Now it is your turn to apply your knowledge of classroom design and start creating your own classroom space.

The following two activities require you to apply what you have learned from this chapter and prior chapters. To begin you will create your own learning environment. You will think about the floor plan, placement of students, and an explanation for your design. The second activity will have you think about the wall space in your classroom. The third activity will have you identify procedures and rules that will help your students use the space safely and efficiently. As you engage in these activities, remember to think about how designing the physical learning space reflects your philosophy for engaging all learners.

Create Your Learning Environment

You will be creating the floor plan for your future classroom along with a rationale justifying your design. To help in this process, you want to clearly address variables that have direct implications for how teachers design.

1. What grade will you be teaching? What are specific items you want to have in your classroom that are developmentally appropriate for that grade level? For example, do you want to have a class carpet, space for manipulative materials, appropriate bookshelves?
2. What subject(s) will you be teaching? What are specific classroom materials that would help support the teaching of that subject? For example, do you need a space to do science labs?
3. How many students do you anticipate having in your classroom? In many school districts, there is a maximum number of students designated for different grade levels. You want to make sure you will have seating options available to all your students.
4. What type of instruction do you see yourself using? Will you be using direct instruction? Facilitative? Group work? Class discussions and debates? Depending on the methods you foresee using in your class, you will want to create a learning space that supports those types of instructional practices.
5. What rules and procedures do you need for this classroom space? Go back to the rules, discipline model, and procedures you created in previous chapters. Update or modify rules and procedures you have constructed; or add new rules and procedures that you believe are needed for your physical classroom that you did not consider before. Make sure your rules and procedures work within this space.

Once you have answered these questions, you will begin designing. Using an online resource, or constructing your floor plan using pencil and paper, begin creating your learning space. Make sure the room aligns with your philosophy. In other words, if you believe collaboration is a central component of your classroom, placing desks in a single file would not resonate with your philosophy. However, having table groups would align to your philosophy. There is no right or wrong, it just needs to align.

You also need to consider your responses to the questions you answered earlier, and make sure your floor plan takes into consideration all of those variables. For example, if you are designing a class for a science classroom that does different labs, you will need to make sure the layout is conducive to doing lab work.

In addition to the floor plan, include pictures or descriptions of items you would want to include that might not be visible in the floor plan. For example, you might want to offer your students alternative seating options. Or you might want to have certain storage bins for table groups. It is important to think about the following: (1) consideration for the materials you want in your classroom that support your instruction, (2) align to different procedures and routines you might have in your class, and (3) make sure your room design gives students opportunities to utilize the classroom space.

After you construct your classroom floor plan write your rationale as to why you designed it the way you did. Explain how you would use the space as a teacher, and how you imagine students using the space and making it their own. Remember, you want this space to foster a sense of community and support the learning of all students.

Don't Forget the Walls

Often teachers only think about the floor design and forget about the wall space when designing the classroom. Wall space is crucial because it can provide additional content information, support rules and procedures, and showcase the wonderful work and talents of the students.

For this activity, you will create three types of wall space.

1. *Academic Support:* This is a visual that represents content that you would be teaching in class. For example, some teachers will have a poster that represents the writing process. That way, students who might be struggling to remember the steps of the writing process could look at the poster. Or, if you are teaching about a historical time period, you might have a timeline on the wall and then students can put different events and people on the timeline with information. The goal is to create a wall space that provides a visual to academic content being learned in class to help students recall information and support a variety of types of learners in your classroom.
2. *Building Class Community:* Building a strong classroom community is the foundation for classroom management, and should be seen through a variety of aspects including the rules, procedures, communication, classroom design, and even the wall space. A great example is having a gallery walk in which each student has a designated space to post work they are proud of. This gives students a chance to show off their hard work, and also see and acknowledge the hard work of their peers. Another idea would be to have a bulletin board for Student of the

Week. The student can bring in pictures and share about him/herself. Each week a different student gets to shine. Having a constant visual reminder around the classroom helps build a class community and reinforces the importance of every student. It is another opportunity for students to become invested in their class.
3. *Supporting Rules and Procedures:* Using wall space to provide visuals to post information about rules and procedures is one way to help remind students and also give students accountability. For example, a teacher might create a poster with a list of the morning routines. It is a helpful reminder for students, as they walk into the classroom, to see posted what they need for the day. A good idea is to pick procedures and create posters with visuals to help students remember to follow the procedure and exactly what to do. It gives students accountability and saves the teacher a lot of time.

Once you have created each type of wall space, you will want to provide a brief description. Describe what it is, and how it supports academics, community building, or class management. For instance, I might provide a poster of a world map and have students identify their ancestry. They would research and describe their ancestry and add it to the wall space designated to build a classroom community. In addition, this aligns to social studies content about community, places, and ancestry.

Having a shared bulletin board is a great way to support visual learners and allow all students to make connections. It is a continual reminder because students see it posted on the walls. The visual might align to my philosophy about building community and giving students ownership by seeing themselves as part of that bulletin board. Once you have created a wall space, you will also want to describe it and support it.

REFERENCES

Brophy, J. E. (1983). Classroom organization and management. *The Elementary School Journal, 83*(4), 265–285.

Bucholz, J. L., & Sheffler, J. L. (2009). Creating a warm and inclusive classroom environment: Planning for all children to feel welcome. *Electronic Journal for Inclusive Education, 2*(4), 4.

Clayton, M. K. (2001). *Classroom spaces that work: Strategies for teachers series.* Northeast Foundation for Children, Greenfield, MA.

Emmer, E. T., Evertson, C. M., & Anderson, L. M. (1980). Effective classroom management at the beginning of the school year. *The Elementary School Journal, 80*(5), 219–231.

Good, T. L., & Power, C. N. (1976). Designing successful classroom environments for different types of students. *Journal of Curriculum Studies, 8*(1), 45–60.

Gremmen, M. C., Van Den Berg, Y. H., Segers, E., & Cillessen, A. H. (2016). Considerations for classroom seating arrangements and the role of teacher characteristics and beliefs. *Social Psychology of Education, 19*(4), 749–774.

Kounin, J., & Sherman, L. (1979). School environments as behavior settings. *Theory into Practice, 18*(3), 145–150.

Miller, D. (2008). *Teaching with intention: Defining beliefs, aligning practice, taking action, K–5*. Stenhouse Publishers.

Responsive Classroom. (2018). *Teaching self-discipline: The Responsive Classroom guide to helping students dream, behave, and achieve in elementary school*. Center for Responsive Schools, Inc.

Rosenfield, P., Lambert, N. M., & Black, A. (1985). Desk arrangement effects on pupil classroom behavior. *Journal of Educational Psychology, 77*(1), 101.

Roskos, K., & Neuman, S. B. (2011). The classroom environment: First, last, and always. *The Reading Teacher, 65*(2), 110–114.

Tate, M. L. (2007). *Shouting won't grow dendrites: 20 techniques for managing a brain-compatible classroom*. Corwin Press.

Tincani, M. J. (2011). *Preventing challenging behavior in your classroom: Positive behavior support and effective classroom management*. Waco, TX: Prufrock Press Inc.

Chapter 6

Collaborating with Families

Families' involvement with and attitude toward education and the school significantly impacts student success, and positive interactions with teachers can help enhance both (Jones & Jones, 2016). This chapter will explore the importance of cultivating open and collaborative relationships with students' families, focusing on ways we can communicate effectively in all situations. We purposefully use the term families to indicate the many individuals who care for and support children in their homes.

FOUNDATION

Having strong collaborative relationships with your students' families can promote academic growth and create a more open, culturally responsive, and equitable environment to support student development (Auerbach, 2015; Jones & Jones, 2016; Noguera, 2001). Teachers must know how to build a cohesive community beyond the classroom by partnering and communicating with families (Auerbach, 2015; Jones & Jones, 2016; LePage et al., 2005).

Creating partnerships with families requires effective communicators sharing important information about classroom events and student academic needs. Additionally, teachers need to be good listeners, hearing and processing what families share, as this is crucial information that impacts teacher's work with their students. All of this requires trust: "Teachers must trust parents and parents must trust teachers" (Kriete, 2005, p. 3),

Cultivating trust with families is complex and takes time and effort. This requires that teachers take a proactive approach that opens spaces for ongoing communication (Auerbach, 2015; Jones & Jones, 2016; Whitaker & Fiore, 2001). However, this is also often "one of the most challenging and potentially unnerving tasks that educators deal with" as part of their work (Whitaker & Fiore, 2001, p. ix). This is especially true when we have more challenging conversations with families or if problems arise at school. While it is understandable that it can be intimidating, this is crucial work that effective teachers initiate even before the school year begins.

While establishing relationships with your students is crucial, we also must cultivate relationships with students' families. As you prepare for the start of a new school year, it is essential to think about how you will communicate and interact with students' families (Davis & Yang, 2005; Jones & Jones, 2016).

We suggest that you develop a comprehensive plan for communication that outlines how you will introduce yourself, communicate information regularly, follow up with a family's question or issue, and ways that you want families to communicate with you. Preparing this ahead of time provides you with an organized approach that you can then share with families to ensure that everyone knows how you will collaborate and support one another throughout the year.

PUTTING IDEAS INTO PRACTICE

Start by thinking about how you will provide a warm welcome to families as partners in their child's learning for the upcoming school year. The teacher's immediate goal is to think about how they can introduce themselves, show that they care for their students and their families, and try to put families at ease. Additionally, this is a crucial time to communicate important information about the grade level, classroom routines, or units of study that the teacher believes are essential for families to know and understand.

Teachers can communicate with families in multiple ways by creating error-free introduction letters, placing individual phone calls, and posting and sharing a video to social media or a class website. Be sure that any method of communication is accessible to all families and that you are providing options for translations or accurate closed captions.

As you communicate with families throughout the school year, your goal is to strengthen your relationship with each student's family. Developing a communication plan will help you consistently keep in touch with families and be prepared to share information with families about ways they can reach out to you. For example, you may share with families at back-to-school night that you will be updating the class website weekly to include new vocabulary or homework information and big ideas about the topics you are exploring as a class.

You want to be transparent with families about how they can contact you and when they might expect to hear back from you. For example, while email is ubiquitous, it is not advisable for you to check email every five minutes as you are trying to teach your class. Instead, let families know when you will be reviewing and returning emails, informing them that they should contact the school office if they need an immediate response. You must ensure that you follow up on emails and phone messages during the times you indicated you would do so.

Today, we often use emails and texts to communicate almost everything. While these forms of communication provide a quick and easy means for sharing information, be mindful of when you believe an actual conversation (in person, on the phone, or virtually) might be a better way to engage in productive communication. Emails often lack a clear tone and can easily create a situation where the intended message is misunderstood.

Be mindful of what you are writing down in emails as those communications become permanent records. It is usually advisable to invite families to meet or talk when you think you need to discuss a matter or if a family needs to understand something that is happening a bit better. Taking the time to meet or talk can help put families at ease and ensure that there is a greater likelihood that there are no miscommunications.

Establishing positive relationships with families will help you when you need to reach out to them to discuss any challenges a student may be facing in your classroom. While it may seem difficult to have challenging conversations with families, when you have established effective relationships, you understand that you are there to work with and support one another to benefit the student.

When engaging in these conversations, it helps to start by noting something positive that you know or have seen the student doing at school. Then you can get into the purpose of your phone call by describing the actions you are noticing in the classroom. Be sure not to label the student or the behavior, just describe what you are observing. Ask some questions to gain the family's perspective and find out what they observe or hear their child saying at home. Seek out a partnership with and support from the family to develop a plan that will help you collectively work with the student. Figure 6.1 gives an example of how you might engage in a conversation about an academic concern.

Figure 6.1. Conversation Example

> Hi! This is Mike Ryan, Jamila's teacher. She brings such joy to our classroom always having something nice to say about her classmates. I wanted to reach out because I have been noticing that Jamila seems to get really frustrated during math lessons. When I work with her one on one, she seems to do a bit better, but when she is working independently, she is really struggling. Have you been noticing this at home with homework? Does she ever say anything about math work?

Challenging conversations are not easy for anyone. Indeed, they can be stressful for the teacher, but remember that families also find the conversations stressful. Many families are often nervous when talking with the teacher, especially if they know that it may be a challenging situation. They may bring previous negative experiences with school to the conversation that can impact their presence. Additionally, families want the best for their children, making these conversations emotional for them, and we need to remember that as teachers.

As you engage in a challenging discussion, either in person, on the phone, or virtually, try to remain neutral and put yourself in their shoes. Ultimately, remember that we are working to form partnerships with families that will enable us to collaborate and help each student grow and develop positively while they are in school.

As you review the scenarios in the next section, think about ways you can apply some of the ideas presented as you engage in the work of a classroom teacher.

Scenario 1: The Challenging Phone Call Message

From time to time, you will hear from parents regarding concerns about their child's academic progress or behavioral issues, which you can address directly. However, at times you will hear from parents with social concerns, and it involves other children. Building the skills that allow you to address these concerns while letting a parent know you hear them, but do not compromise the privacy of other children or your professional decisions that you know are best for building classroom community is essential. The following scenario encourages you to think about this type of situation.

You are a second grade teacher at University Elementary School. Bruno Ortiz and Shayna Johnson are both students in your classroom. Bruno has been exhibiting some behavioral challenges in the classroom for the last few months. He can be pretty handsy and requires that you stop and redirect him frequently. At times he has spit at other students. You have been working with administrators and other school faculty to try and address Bruno's needs. Shayna is a very bright and with-it student. You have often asked her to be a partner (almost a role model) with Bruno, and they work quite well together. Shayna also often asks if she can work with Bruno, and frequently the two will play together during recess.

In the past, you have met with Shayna's family to discuss their concerns about her academic progress. They feel as if Shayna is a gifted reader and should be challenged more. While Shayna is a great "word" reader, she often rushes and does not always fully comprehend what she has read. Additionally, she is challenged when asked to think critically about a text. You are working on these things with Shayna and some of her peers during small group and independent reading time.

You received the following voicemail message from Shayna's family yesterday evening on your school phone:

We want to talk to you about Shayna and that student Bruno. She tells us that you always make her partner with him, and WE WANT IT TO STOP! We do not understand why he is even in your class and feel you need to do a much better job of managing his behavior. We also need to talk with you about Shayna's progress as we feel she has not been sufficiently challenged this year. We expect to hear back from you by the end of the day tomorrow with solutions.

After listening to the voice message, you know you must respond. However, before you call Shayna's family, you want to prepare some talking points. Try to think about what you want to accomplish. In preparation, try to address the following prompts:

- How would you start that conversation?
- What would be important for you to say and communicate to Shayna's family?
- What challenges do you foresee in that conversation? How would you handle those difficult questions or comments?
- What specific ideas would you want to suggest during the conversation?
- How would you like to end the conversation?
- What follow-up could you imagine having with the parents, administration, and support staff after the conversation?

Scenario 2: Parent Volunteer Email

It takes a village to support an early elementary classroom. Volunteers become a great way of getting an extra set of hands to help young learners. These programs need to be managed carefully by the classroom teacher, requiring clear communication about expectations and how volunteers should interact with students and each other. Managing people in your classroom creates additional communication needs, especially when you need to address an issue you observe or if the volunteer brings up a situation that requires attention. The following scenario gets you to think about one of these types of problems.

Scenario:

Jamie is a kindergarten teacher with twenty-eight students in her class. Mrs. Thompson is Jamie's full-time paraprofessional who assists with the classroom. Jamie has decided to welcome families into the classrooms to assist with centers to ensure that there are enough hands to help with all her students.

After sending out an email requesting help along with a hard copy request, Jamie received a few responses from family members who were willing and able to come and assist in the classroom. From that initial response, four classroom volunteers, Mrs. Plum, Ms. Santino, Mr. Stanley, and Dr. Fancy indicated they could regularly come to assist with centers.

It has been a month since Mrs. Plum, Ms. Santino, Mr. Stanley, and Dr. Fancy have been coming into the classroom to help during center time. Jamie has arranged for four core centers and two instructional centers, one led by Mrs. Thompson and one by Jamie. Things seemingly have been going along very well, and Jamie feels as if the volunteers are helping to ensure that her students have opportunities for more personalized attention. They allow her to plan for more engaging center activities.

One Friday, Jamie received an email from Ms. Santino, depicted in figure 6.2.

Figure 6.2.   Parent Email

To: Jamie Stern

From: Angela Santino

Re: This Week at Centers

Ms. Stern,

Another great week with the kiddos. I wanted to write to you because I noticed that Andre has really been giving you a hard time in class, not following directions and disobeying your directions. Mrs. Thompson was telling me that this happens all day long. It must be so frustrating. I know that today Andre refused to make happy eyes for his turkey and just put his head down on the table.

In fact, Tina (Ms. Santino's daughter) was telling me about how mean Andre is during recess, refusing to play with the other students. The class parents and I have talked about this too, he's really not fitting in with the rest of the class. What can we do to help him out? Is it true that his mother was just sent to prison? Mrs. Thompson mentioned that and I think that is absolutely terrible. Let me know what we can do.

Best,

Angie

Jamie was surprised and annoyed at this email and struggled to think about a way to respond. Take some time to suggest a way that Jamie could effectively reply to this email. As you process your response, keep the following questions in mind:

- What is essential to know about how Jamie established her volunteer program and communicated with all the volunteers?
- What roles should a paraprofessional and volunteers play in a classroom?

- What are key things to note about this email from Ms. Santino?
- Describe the process you would use to respond to Ms. Santino and how you would reply to this email.

"TEACHER TALK": PRACTICAL STRATEGIES FROM EXPERIENCED TEACHERS

Teachers are fantastic resources. You will learn a great deal from colleagues once you begin your career, and they will also learn new ideas from you. It is helpful to seek out and listen to other teachers' advice to grow and enhance your work. The following three teachers each have many years of experience. They are sharing tips and strategies for communicating with families. Read the following and think about what might work for you. In the next section, you will begin to apply their ideas as you create and develop your own communication materials.

Teacher Talk 1

I begin each school year by reaching out individually to families of the children in my class on the first day of school. During this first communication, I share my excitement to begin to know their family and an example of how their child engaged with the class community on the first day. Initiating dialogue that is positive and student-centered often lays a strong foundation for open dialogue with families throughout the school year and communicates to families that I am here to support their child. For this message to be most effective, it is essential to make initial contact with families on or as close to the first day of school as possible. This helps ensure that my first message to each family is a positive one and that it occurs before I may need to contact a family with difficult news.

These initial phone calls and emails have led to families sharing essential information about their child sooner than they may have otherwise, allowing me to more effectively help each child experience a successful start to the year. Upon hearing from me on the first day of school, many families are happy to have gained a small snapshot into their child's first day. Families have expressed that they were nervous about how their child would experience their first day in a new class community and that hearing from the teacher put some of their concerns to rest. The first day of school presents many demands on a teacher's time but setting aside time to contact each family on day one pays dividends for me throughout the school year and in years to come.

—Teacher Christine Prestiane

Teacher Talk 2

As a teacher with twenty-five years of experience, I have always found great value in parent–teacher communication. While it has looked different over the years, it has always been an important part of my philosophy, and I have taken pride in doing it. In sharing my thoughts on this topic, I hope that new teachers will also find the benefits to establishing their method of communication with their students' families.

Regardless of the format or method of communication, in my experience, I have always found that parents appreciate knowing what is going on in their child's classroom as it helps them to feel connected. We all know that when asked how their day was at school and what they learned, the average elementary school student is likely to give a one-word answer. From S'More to SeeSaw to a Weebly webpage to just an old-fashioned email or printed newsletter, find a way that works for you to inform parents of what's going on in your classroom.

I believe in a weekly update that includes a brief overview of the curriculum covered, homework assignments, upcoming assessments, and special classroom or school-wide activities. Reminders about school functions, PTO meetings, or school spirit days can also be included. In my experience, the more specific to your own classroom, the better.

At the beginning of each school year, I always like to send out a "get to know the teacher" page to introduce myself to my students and their families. There are many ideas and templates for these on Pinterest, Teacher Blogs, and Teachers Pay Teachers. I like to share a little bit about myself; my educational background, my family, and some of my favorite things, such as hobbies, books, musicians, color, food, and so on. At this time, I also invite families to write me a letter or send me an email to tell me a little more about their child, their strengths and weaknesses, likes and dislikes, and anything else their parent feels would help me get to know their child better.

Depending upon the makeup of your student population, you may need to have more flexibility in your communication. Consider sending home a hard copy of your emailed weekly newsletter for families without access to a computer or email. If you have Spanish-speaking families, consider using an online translation service to translate your weekly newsletter. While this is not always 100 percent accurate, I have always found that these families appreciate the effort. Typically, I would also send the newsletter in English to these families, as there may be an older child capable of reading it to the mom and or dad.

While it may seem like one more thing to do each week, in the long run, you will find that there is an upside to weekly communication. By establishing an open line of communication and setting this routine, you will often find you are not as bombarded with parent emails and questions. It also helps to create a rapport between home and school. You may even find that your school district or building principal has made this a focus and an expectation.

—Teacher Christine Hindman

Teacher Talk 3

Emailing parents is the most proactive and effective form of communication as an upper elementary school teacher. It allows me to keep in constant contact with all families. It can also be an easy way to contact parents/guardians since synching teacher/family schedules can often be complex. Additionally, for those families that may struggle with the English language, being able to copy and paste my email text into Google Translate or other translation applications allows them to have a better grasp on our classroom happenings.

I communicate with parents at the beginning of the year and throughout the entire year using email. I start the year off by collecting all parent/guardian emails and creating a group email address. I title the group email address with a general name and school year, such as "Parents/Guardians 2021–2022." This allows me to quickly access all parents/guardians at one time when I want to disseminate information.

I use email for various reasons. I start the year by introducing myself, my classroom expectations, and sending links to beginning-of-year activities and fun quizzes. Throughout the year, I use email to provide my families with updates on upcoming projects, field trips, important assessments, school news, and so forth. I also use it to provide links to various resources that parents/guardians can utilize with their children, such as Scholastic Book order reminders, reinforcement resources such as Mystery Science links, and teacher-created videos. Student-created classroom videos/projects and photo links of the children doing creative or fun projects in school are also shared through my parent/guardian email chain.

There are weeks when I may reach out to my parents several times in one week, or there may be times when I go longer than a couple of weeks before needing to reach out for whole-class emails. If I need to reach out to individuals or smaller groups of parents, I can also do that whenever I need to. I usually do this when I need to remind a family of something that may need to be handed in, if there is missing homework that needs to be addressed, or if I need to set up a time to speak with a parent/guardian regarding a specific child's needs, behavior, or just to send a positive shout-out! Sending a positive email to highlight a particular honor or goal, for example, that a student has achieved is always a cause for celebration; emailing is a quick, easy, and much-appreciated way to reach out and share!

I constantly have parents comment on how much they appreciate the regular updates they receive from me through email. It allows me to be more proactive than reactive to situations or topics of conversation. Finally, parents are better able to help and support each other and their children when they are all receiving the same message simultaneously, and we are all on the same page together.

—Teacher Theresa Pignataro

IT'S YOUR TURN: CREATE

You have learned some of the foundations of communicating with families, thought through challenging case studies, and learned strategies from practicing teachers. Now it is time to build your communication toolbox. Teachers can prepare resources to help develop communication. In this activity section, you will work to build your own. Follow the different prompts to create your communication tools. Keep in mind, these will change and constantly evolve to meet the individual nature of your classroom and school community each year.

Create an Introduction Letter in Multiple Languages

Begin by creating your introduction letter that you would send and share with students and their families before the school year begins or on the first day of school. You want this letter to be professional while still providing a small piece of your personal life, so students and families feel connected. Your letter should include the following:

- Show your personal side as a way to connect. For example, if you have children or a pet. Or you might share where you are from or places you have traveled. Make sure the personal touches are appropriate and keep them short.
- Preview what students will learn this year. You want to get students excited about learning, so share one or two projects or units of study that will be fun and engaging. For example, you might communicate that during the first marking period, all students will get to pick a historical figure, use different forms of technology to research that person, and

then have the opportunity to dress and act as that person at the annual class wax museum.
- Remember, this is just a quick preview and way to get students and families excited. You do not want to overwhelm them.
- Finally, and most importantly, you want to share how excited you are to meet each student and create a fun and welcoming learning environment. Every student and parent should walk away feeling excited about the start of the year.

Now that you have created the introduction letter in your native language, you need to think about how this letter could be translated for all your families. You might find a colleague, family member, or friend who speaks/writes in a different language who can help you translate. Or go to the school and ask if there are personnel or other resources to help with translations. You can also find resources online to help you translate documents.

Your task for this activity is to create your introductory letter and get it translated into one other language.

Create a Weekly or Monthly Newsletter

Remember, the class community extends beyond the four walls of your classroom. Communicating with your families regularly is vital for expanding your community from school to home. Regular communication should be weekly or monthly, and it should be based on what you can commit to and accomplish. Remember, teachers have a lot to do, and time is one of your most valuable commodities. If you can provide a weekly newsletter, you can and should. If you can only provide a monthly newsletter, that also works. Whichever you choose to do is excellent; just clearly communicate that to your families at the beginning of the year. That way, they know to expect it, and they can look forward to receiving it.

Your weekly or monthly newsletter should accomplish the following three goals:

1. Highlight the great things students have been learning and doing in the classroom. For example, share about the class presentations the students just gave. Or congratulate the families on students finishing their first math test.
2. Prepare families for what students will learn and do in the classroom during the next week or month. For example, if you are starting a new unit of study, you should share information about the content and what students will be learning. Or if students will be reading fiction books and doing some great activities, talk a little bit about it. You might even

want to share some ideas for what parents could ask at home to extend the conversation.
3. Finally, share any logistical information that needs to be communicated with families. For example, if there is a PTO meeting or announcements. Or if there is an event coming up at school. Or, if any forms need to be completed, it is great to communicate this in the newsletter. Some teachers might even provide a little calendar to help.

Now it is your turn to create. Create a weekly or monthly newsletter that you would send home. Remember to meet all three goals as you create this. You might also go back to the Teacher Talk section and read some of their suggestions for what to include in a newsletter. Remember, your newsletter needs to be professional.

Create a Parent Questionnaire or Survey

Richard Rogers and Oscar Hammerstein might have written it best in their song "Getting to Know You," when a new schoolteacher tells their students that the most important thing is getting to know their pupils. Part of getting to know your students is getting to know their families and learning from them about their children. Parent questionnaires and surveys are a fantastic way to do this. Questionnaires and surveys can accomplish two goals: (1) learning about the student and (2) learning about the families.

To learn about the student, you want to ask questions that give insight into who they are at home to help you as a teacher. For example, what interests do they have, and what activities do they participate in outside of school? Questions like these are non-academic but give important information into who they are as a person. You also want to ask academic questions, such as what subject does your child enjoy most? What learning goals do you have for your child this school year? As you ask these questions, it is essential to remember that you are learning about the student from the parent's perspective. How the parent sees their child at home and outside the classroom might be different from what you experience in the school.

In addition to learning about the student, you also want a few questions about the families. This way, you can better understand the home learning environment by asking questions such as who lives in the home (i.e., siblings, grandparents, etc.)? Or what language(s) are spoken at home? Keeping in mind that there is no set model of a family and understanding what happens at home can help understand how students behave in the classroom, work with their peers, and interact with you. Additionally, know more about students' families will help you best understand the rich diversity in your classroom and enable you to make all students feel recognized and included rather than marginalized.

Now it is your turn. Create a questionnaire or survey that you would send home to families at the beginning of the school year. Keep it between five and ten questions. It should meet the following criteria:

1. Learn about who the child is at home and outside of the school (i.e., activities, hobbies, sports, musical interests, etc.).
2. Learn about the academic and social goals the parent has for the school year.
3. Learn a little about the family and the child's home life so you can make a connection.

Questionnaires and surveys are a wonderful way to learn more about your students through the parents' eyes. It also helps you create a foundation for working with parents and families, which will benefit you as you continue through the school year.

Create Volunteer Materials

Teachers are wonderful at utilizing their resources. Resources include parents and families. In your questionnaire and survey, you might ask families how they would like to participate in the classroom. Some families might be willing to come into the classroom. Others might be able to help outside of the school. While some families might be hesitant to help, which is also okay, you want to let them know that they are always welcome.

Some ways families can volunteer include:

1. **Academic Support:** This might be coming into the classroom and doing a read-aloud or helping with small group work. Or, if you are putting together a project, parents might come in to help students as they work on their projects. Families can also support without coming into the class. For example, if you have students creating published books, you might ask parents to help with the publishing process, which could be done at home.
2. **Classroom Beautification Support:** Ask families to come in and help with creating spaces for students. You might need help with a bulletin board or the classroom library. These are great ways to get parents involved.
3. **Academic and Social Celebrations:** Families might want to come in to experience some of the activities students are doing. For example, if you have a wax museum, science fair, or other student presentations,

you will want to invite families to come in and watch. It is an excellent way for parents and families to be part of academic achievements. You might also invite families to come in during holidays or other school-wide celebrations. Suppose parents cannot physically come into the classroom. In that case, you might think about ways families can attend virtually so they can also be part of these wonderful academic and social celebrations.

Inviting families to participate in your classroom, either in-person or at home, is a fantastic way of building a community. However, it takes some work and organization from you, the teacher. You want to think about how you are informing families and your expectations for each of these types of volunteer activities.

For this activity, you are going to create a flyer. It is up to you to make this for a specific event (i.e., science fair, holiday celebration, help with bulletin boards, etc.). Create an invitation flyer that clearly describes the activity families will attend. After you describe the event or activity, clearly communicate your expectations. For example, you might say you are looking for help every Monday for one hour to help organize the classroom library. Or you might say you are hosting the science fair and you need help with the following jobs, and then clearly state each assignment and the time commitment. Once you have described the event and your expectations, you want to write how parents and families can volunteer to participate.

In addition to creating this sample flyer, you might also want to create a flyer to go out with your "beginning of the school year letter." This new flyer would show families different opportunities to get involved. Be creative with this. It is a great way to get families excited about the school year and feel like they are also part of your classroom.

Create Friendly Academic Information for Families

Hundreds of students go home every day and are asked, "What did you learn in school today?" Families often hear: "Nothing," or "I don't remember," or "I don't know." Another common scenario is when families are helping their child at home complete homework, but the child says, "That is not how we learned to do it." This often leaves families and children frustrated and unsure of how to do the work.

To reduce these situations, teachers might consider creating academic-friendly information that helps families at home. One idea is to create short videos that you can send to families showing what you are doing in class. Or video tapping a read-aloud that parents can then watch with their child at home.

For this activity, you will create a short video. A video should be no more than five minutes. The video should only be of you; never include children in your video since you will be sharing it with the entire class. Begin the video with a friendly welcome and clearly stating the goal. For example, in this video, I will be sharing how we learned to regroup in math class using manipulatives. Once you have clearly stated the goal, then give your demonstration. After that, you can leave students and parents with a discussion question. For example, suppose you did a read-aloud to highlight the lesson on figurative language. In that case, you might ask families and students to talk to each other and share different examples of figurative language from the book.

Creating these short videos are a great way to extend what you are doing in the classroom to the home. Remember, these should always be optional. Families should not feel compelled to watch or participate. These should just be a fun way to help families feel connected.

REFERENCES

Auerbach, S. (2015). Fantastic family collaboration. In Murawski, W. & Scott, L. (Eds.). *What really works in elementary education*. Thousand Oaks: Corwin

Davis, C., & Yang, A. (2005). *Parents & teachers working together*. Northeast Foundation for Children.

Jones, V. F., & Jones, L. S. (2016). *Comprehensive classroom management: Creating communities of support and solving problems*. Pearson.

Kriete, R. (2005). Introduction: Opening the door to families. In Davis, C., & Yang, A. (Eds.). *Parents & teachers working together*. Northeast Foundation for Children.

LePage, P.; Darling-Hammond, L.; Akar, H.; Gutierrez, E.; Jenkins-Gunn, E.; & Rosebrock, K. (2005). Classroom management. In Darling-Hammond, L., & Bransford, J. (Eds.). *Preparing teachers for a changing world: What teachers should learn and be able to do*. John Wiley & Sons.

Noguera, P. (2001). Transforming urban schools through investments in the social capital of parents. In M. Warren (Ed.). *Social capital in poor communities*. New York: Russell Sage Foundation.

Whitaker, T., & Fiore, D. (2001). *Dealing with difficult parents and with parents in difficult situations*. New York: Eye on Education.

Chapter 7

Self-Care

Managing Yourself

Teaching is a rewarding profession, however it can be incredibly stressful. The stress of this work can be overwhelming and cause exhaustion and burnout (Garner, Bender, & Fedor, 2018; Jennings et al., 2017; Zarate, Maggin, & Passmore, 2019). A teacher's mental and emotional state has a great impact on classroom climate as well as student learning. This highlights another significant impact of teacher stress (Armstrong, 2019; Frank et al., 2015; Jennings et al., 2017).

It is crucial for teachers to find ways to care for themselves and develop effective techniques for dealing with the stress in healthy and productive ways (Fabbro et al., 2020; Garner et al., 2018; Jennings et al., 2017; Lucas, 2017; Zarate et al., 2019). This chapter presents some information on the impacts of stress and how developing self-care techniques can help to reduce these challenges. Additionally, readers are presented with some ideas and suggestions they can use to try and manage their own emotions and stress.

FOUNDATION

Teacher stress, mental and emotional health, and overall burnout are major factors in many teachers deciding to leave the profession (Garner, Bender, & Fedor, 2018; Jennings et al., 2017; Zarate, Maggin, & Passmore, 2019). The expectations of the work as well as the level of emotional connections needed to navigate everyday life in schools require that teachers develop strong social and emotional competencies (Garner et al., 2018; Jennings et al., 2017; Lucas, 2017; Zarate et al., 2019). These competencies help teachers to deal effectively with the emotional challenges and stress of teaching life as well as make sure they are emotionally available to tend to the needs of their students (Armstrong, 2019; Frank et al., 2015; Lucas, 2017; Jennings et al., 2017).

Teachers who lack strong social and emotional competencies negatively impact classroom climate and student learning (Armstrong, 2019; Frank et al., 2015; Jennings et al., 2017). This in turn impacts the ways in which teachers can effectively manage their classrooms. Teachers with well-developed social and emotional regulation skills tend to build more positive relationships as well as have better classroom management (Frank et al., 2015; Jennings et al., 2017; Zarate et al., 2019).

Developing mindfulness practices has helped teachers to develop the social and emotional skills necessary to manage the many academic, social, and emotional stressors they face each day (Armstrong, 2019; Fabbro et al., 2020; Garner et al., 2018; Jennings et al., 2017; Lucas, 2017; Zarate et al., 2019). Mindfulness can be defined as the ways in which individuals tune in to everyday moment to moment situations nonjudgmentally, with curiosity and openness (Fabbro et al., 2020; Garner et al., 2018; Jennings et al., 2017; Zarate et al., 2019).

Mindful practices allow teachers to observe, accept, and adapt to their emotions, causing them to reduce anxiety and emotional exhaustion (Fabbro et al., 2020; Garner et al., 2018; Jennings et al., 2017; Zarate et al., 2019). When teachers employ effective mindfulness practices as a form of self-care, they are examining the moments of their daily lives with intentionality allowing them to better process and regulate emotional pressures and job (and/or life) stress (Garner et al., 2018; Jennings et al., 2017; Lucas, 2017; Zarate et al., 2019).

There are many different mindful practices that teachers can employ to ensure that they are caring for their well-being (Armstrong, 2019; Garner et al., 2018; Jennings et al., 2017; Lucas, 2017). Individuals need to try different practices to find the one(s) that work best for them. Mindful practices can include meditation, breathing exercises, simply taking a walk, listening to music, exercising, or anything that helps one slow down and process emotions objectively (Armstrong, 2019; Lucas, 2017; Zarate et al., 2019). Additional mindful activities that promote self-care encourage teachers to look at what they are doing each day and make a priorities list, focusing on accomplishing essential tasks and identifying anything that is not necessary. This will ensure their work is accomplished and students are learning (Lucas, 2017).

It is also important that teachers are tending to their personal needs, especially ensuring that they are making time for adequate sleep as well as getting proper nutrition (Lucas, 2017). Ultimate mindful practices help individuals better deal with the challenges of their work in schools as well as ensure that they maintain focus on what is important. No one can expect these practices to work immediately or to prevent or correct everything that causes them social or emotional stress (Armstrong, 2019). As people engage in these self-care practices they need practice, finding that over time being mindful can make a positive impact and help them to develop more positive habits of mind (Armstrong, 2019; Fabbro et al. 2020).

PUTTING IDEAS INTO PRACTICE

Every teacher experiences the social and emotional stress of the teaching profession. Given the many demands being placed on teachers from testing requirements, communicating with families, maintaining professional relations with colleagues to the daily pressures of managing and running a classroom, it is crucial to have a self-care plan. Self-care is the way in which an individual works to ensure that they are meeting their daily responsibilities while ensuring their social, emotional, and physical well-being.

People talk about or suggest different ideas designed to support self-care; however, there is no one, single suggestion that will satisfy every individual. Each teacher needs to identify the practices that will help him or her to best manage personal well-being. That being said, *all* teachers need to look at some of their physical practices to ensure that they are getting sufficient sleep, nutrition, and some exercise. These practices help to support a healthy body, which is the first step in addressing personal well-being.

There are many practices that individuals can choose to help combat the stressors of teaching. Practicing self-care allows individuals to accomplish all required tasks in a timely manner while ensuring they are meeting their physical, social, and emotional needs. Teachers have a lot of work to support their students properly, therefore it is crucial that teachers prioritize their work. Prioritizing your work means that an individual is looking to identify the tasks that are essential and creating a timeline to accomplish all tasks.

When teachers prioritize their work, they look to identify any tasks they may have "created" that are truly not necessary, focusing first on those things that must be accomplished. For example, when report cards are due, it is best to focus on finishing and submitting grades rather than taking time to change bulletin board borders. Additionally, teachers can look at any practices they have that may serve as "time robbers" rather than "time savers." This helps to ensure that teachers are meeting their obligations and streamlining the work they are doing each day.

Once teachers have created a structure for their daily work, they can start to look at personal practices that will address their social and emotional well-being. For many individuals, incorporating exercise regularly helps to combat any emotional challenges or stress.

It is also important for teachers to provide themselves with the gift of some solitude during the workday when possible. Taking a brief break allows a teacher to stop, breathe, and reflect on everything that has been happening during the school day. This can help to provide some relief from the fast pace of school life. Teachers can also provide themselves with some solitude by establishing solid boundaries for their work time and personal time. For example, it is clear that emails, texts, and social media have consumed a great deal of time in both personal and professional lives.

As a teacher, one must respond to emails and messages; however, it is not necessary to be checking and responding twenty-four hours a day, seven days a week. Frame out times when you will be checking, responding to messages, or posting information. It is crucial to communicate that with families and students up front. Have an "out of office" message set up during those times that reinforces when one might expect to get a reply. Providing this framework will help you separate your professional and personal times.

Practicing self-care also means ensuring that teachers stay connected with others. Maintaining or cultivating professional relationships helps teachers share ideas, information, and advice with one another. This helps to reinforce the idea that all teachers are facing many common stressors as part of their work. Furthermore, individuals want to ensure that they are taking time to support their personal connections and relationships.

Teachers must provide themselves with time to enjoy personal interests and hobbies. It could be as simple as giving oneself time each night to read a book by a favorite author that has nothing to do with teaching or education. Maintaining outside connections and interests helps to support a personal balance, recognizing that life exists outside the school building. It can be too easy to get completely consumed by work and work issues, but when individuals have outside connections, this helps to provide them with much-needed time away from the demands and stressors of the classroom.

Many individuals also will engage in mindfulness practices to support self-care. Mindfulness practices can help people better understand their own emotional states as well as emotional triggers. These practices help teachers become more aware of themselves, their feelings, and their needs in the moment. This can help individuals better focus on what is happening and crucially important in a particular moment.

Mindfulness practices can include but are not limited to breathing exercises, meditation, yoga, going for a walk to feel the warmth of the sun, enjoying a sip of water or a hot beverage, focusing on noticing the way one's body is feeling and reacting, or maintaining a personal journal. Moreover, when individuals look to practice mindfulness, they take time to unplug from all the electronic devices that consume so much time and personal energy in daily life. They also look to take time to smile, laugh, play, and maintain a sense of personal balance.

The following are some resources teachers can explore if they are looking to develop or support mindfulness practices:

- The Calm App or Website: https://www.calm.com
- Headspace App: https://www.headspace.com
- "How to Meditate" from the *New York Times*: https://www.nytimes.com/guides/well/how-to-meditate
- Mindful: https://www.mindful.org/how-to-practice-mindfulness/
- The Balance App: https://www.balanceapp.com/

Remember that it is important to try some different practices to find the one(s) that meet an individual's needs. Equally as important is giving these practices some time and commitment before giving up. As people develop mindfulness skills, they are learning to quiet themselves physically and mentally. This does not happen overnight and requires practice and commitment.

Processing Practice Exercise 1: Prioritizing

Self-care does not mean picking and choosing which professional tasks a teacher decides to accomplish. All professional tasks need to be accomplished; however, a teacher can learn to prioritize tasks and ask for help to complete certain tasks. Identifying which professional responsibilities must be accomplished immediately and which tasks have leeway in how and when they are completed is an important skill for every teacher to develop.

In this activity, you will help new teacher Ms. Levi prioritize her professional tasks and begin to give suggestions that would help Ms. Levi develop her own management plan. You will be given information about Ms. Levi professionally and personally. You will also be given a timeline of her day, and different professional tasks she needs to accomplish.

The first piece of evidence from Ms. Levi is her responses to a series of questions. She was asked the questions to gauge a little more about her personally and professionally. As you review Ms. Levi's responses (see table 7.1), answer the following questions:

1. What do you think are Ms. Levi's personal priorities?
2. What do you think are Ms. Levi's professional priorities?
3. Do you think there are things Ms. Levi prioritizes professionally that could be changed or modified in some way to give her more personal time? If so, describe.
4. If you were Ms. Levi's friend, what are one or two suggestions or advice you have for her?

Now that you have listened to Ms. Levi share about her personal and professional life, you are going to learn a little more about her daily work responsibilities. Table 7.2 shows Ms. Levi's daily work schedule. She is

Table 7.1. Sample Teacher Survey Questions and Response

Survey Question	Ms. Levi's Response
Do you wake up early or prefer to sleep in?	I wake up early around 5:30 a.m. to walk my dog. I like to take a long walk in the morning since I am gone all day. After my walk, I make my lunch, get ready for school, and leave the house. I usually get to school around 7:30 a.m.
Do you stay up late? Do you like to work late?	I do stay up late, but I do not like to do work after dinner. Sometimes, I must finish my lessons if they are not ready for the next day, or complete grading. I really prefer not to work at night, though I will check and respond to emails.
Do you prefer to do your work at school or would you be okay bringing home work?	I prefer to do all my work at school, but since I have a dog, I try to leave right at 3:30 so that I can get home and walk my dog. I really can't stay later. While I prefer to do my work at school, I do not mind working at home. However, I do not like grading at home. Student work can get heavy and taking it back and forth is very burdensome. I do it because I cannot get it all done at school, although I really do not like carrying all that work back and forth.
What do you do during your prep time?	During my morning prep time I usually spend that time getting materials ready for the day. I am usually in the office making copies or in my room pulling material. Since I usually do my lesson planning at night, I need the next morning to get it all ready for the day. If I have extra time, I try to spend time organizing the room, doing bulletin boards. I find I need to do the things that I cannot bring home with me. I really do not enjoy that type of stuff, but it is important to the students so I try to make it important to me. During my lunch prep I spend half the time in the teacher's lounge talking with other teachers. It is a nice social time. Then I go back to my room and try to grade student work so I don't have to take it all home with me to grade. I really don't like bringing work home.
Do you collaborate with other teachers?	I talk a lot with the other teachers, though it is mostly social. We will sometimes share worksheets. We also talk about the lessons we are doing because we need to be in the same unit of study. However, we do not really plan together or share lesson plans. I think there is a little competitive feeling. If it would help save time, I wouldn't mind planning the social studies lessons. I love social studies. If we could share and someone else could plan science and math lessons that would be ideal. Unfortunately, cooperative planning isn't really the culture of the school.

Do you have any volunteers in your classroom?	No. My parents have asked to help, but I am not sure what they could do. I have also been asked if I want to take a field student from a local university. That seems like it might be more work for me, and I do not have time. If I have volunteers, I am just not sure what to have them do or when to have them come in.
When do you respond to parents' phone calls or emails?	Whenever I can, I always check before and after school with the main office to see if a parent called. I usually call back at that time. I also check emails before and after school and try to respond right away. I check my email during my preps and throughout the day. If there is a down time, I will respond. I check it throughout the evening and respond. I have told my parents that I will not make any phone calls from home, but I will respond to emails. I try to limit my responses during the weekend, though I usually check it once in the morning and evening, just in case there is something very important. I teach at a school where the parents are very involved. There seems to be an unspoken expectation from the parents that I respond within the day. The parents are great. They want to help. They want to know what is going on with their children on a regular basis. Again, that is great, but it can be a little much at times.
What do you do for fun? In the past, what are things you have done for fun?	I don't have much time for fun. I guess walking my dog is what I do for enjoyment every day. I do like to go out to dinner with friends, or go to town in the evenings, if I have time. However, I am usually doing lesson planning or grading in the evenings. I do enjoy reading. I only seem to read in the summertime when I have free time. Before I started teaching, I would paint. I am not very good, but it is enjoyable. In college I belonged to a painting club that would meet at different places on campus and paint. It was fun.
List Your Ongoing Professional Tasks (besides instruction)	Daily: • Lesson Plans (math, science, social studies, reading, & writing) • Prep Materials for Lessons (all subjects) • Grade Student Work • Input Student Grades into Computer • Respond to Parent Emails and Phone Calls • Classroom Beautification and Organization Weekly: • Read and Prepare for School Professional Development and Professional Learning Communities (PLC) • Write Weekly Newsletter As Arise • Attend, Prepare, and Write for IEP Meetings • Prep for School Events (back-to-school, conferences, assemblies, etc.) • Review Curricula and Standards

contracted between the hours of 8:00 a.m. and 3:30 p.m. She usually arrives at school at 7:30 a.m. to get some work done in the morning in preparation for her first class. Ms. Levi tends to leave school at 3:30 p.m. so she can walk her dog.

The table provides a detailed schedule of her day. Some of the items are flexible and can be moved around. Since Ms. Levi teaches math, science, social studies, reading, and writing to her homeroom class; she does have the luxury of determining when those are taught during the day as long as she is still meeting the required minutes for those subjects. Ms. Levi cannot move around the start and end of school. She also cannot move around specials, lunch, or recess.

It is your job to look at her day and take into consideration the information she shared in the survey to see if you can find ways to give her suggestions by answering the following questions:

1. Could Ms. Levi adjust anything in her schedule to give her more time to accomplish some of her professional tasks?
2. Who could Ms. Levi ask to help her accomplish some professional tasks? Be specific about who she could ask, what tasks she could ask them to do, and when the help could take place. For example, could she ask parents to volunteer? If so, what could the parent help do? Or could she ask another teacher to collaborate when it comes to writing lessons? Be creative.
3. Ms. Levi mentioned she must leave at 3:30 p.m. and that she cannot accomplish everything during the school day. What professional tasks would you suggest Ms. Levi take home with her and which tasks and responsibilities should remain at school?
4. What advice or suggestions do you have for Ms. Levi?

Now that you have thought about Ms. Levi and given her suggestions, it is important to think about yourself. Take a few minutes to think about the professional tasks you will need to accomplish as a teacher. Think about those tasks in which you might ask for help and other tasks that you will need to complete yourself. Think about how you will prioritize your professional tasks. Think about where and when you want to do most of your professional work (at home, at school, in the morning, after school, etc.). Remember to consider what personal responsibilities you have, and activities you like to do just for fun. Ask yourself how those personal responsibilities and fun activities will fit into your professional day. Keep these ideas in mind as you move through the rest of the chapter.

Table 7.2. Sample Schedule

Professional/Contracted Schedule

Time	School Activity
8:00	Students Start to Arrive—Students do their morning tasks and then have free time
8:20	School Officially Begins—Morning Meeting
8:45	Math
9:45	Specials (Ms. Levi's Prep)
10:30	Silent Reading
10:45	Reading Lesson and Centers
11:30	Lunch and Recess (Ms. Levi's Lunch and Prep)
12:30	Class Read Aloud
12:45	Writing Lesson
1:15	Free Choice Learning Centers
1:30	Social Studies
2:00	Science
2:30	Free Choice Learning Center (extra time if lessons go long)
2:45	Pack Up for Dismissal
3:00	Dismissal
3:00–3:30	Professional Development Activities *(i.e., grade group meetings, subject group meetings, meetings about students, school-wide meetings, etc.)*

Processing Practice Exercise 2: Interview

Self-care is personal. What works for one person does not always work for someone else. You can learn from the experiences of teachers. Sometimes, you might hear an idea from a teacher that really resonates with you, and you decide to give it a try. Other times, you might hear an idea that works for a teacher, but in the back of your mind you know it would not work for you. Hearing ideas that you do not like is just as important as hearing suggestions that you do like.

In this activity, you are going to interview a teacher. It can be a current or retired teacher. It can be someone who just started teaching, or who has been doing it for years. It is your choice. Ask this person to speak with you for approximately an hour to answer a series of ten questions.

As you ask these questions you can keep a few general notes. Remember, the important thing is really to listen and engage in the interview, not to take notes. As you ask each question you might then have a follow-up question. That is great and you should feel confident asking it.

This is your chance to listen and learn about how a teacher maintains the challenges of a work-life balance. Remember, there are no right or wrong answers to these questions. You might like some ideas, pieces of advice and suggestions that the teacher gives, and you might not. Try not to judge the teacher's answers, but instead just take it all in and learn.

1. What time do you get to school, and what time do you leave school?
2. Do you do all your work at school, or do you take work home with you?
3. What do you do during your prep time?
   a. Do you spend this time alone or do you get together and work with other teachers?
   b. Is this a choice or is it predetermined?
   c. Do you have any advice on how you spend your prep time?
4. What do you do during lunch?
   a. Do you do work and have lunch at the same time?
   b. Do you pause doing work and just enjoy lunch?
   c. Do you spend this time with other teachers or are you alone?
5. What do you do for enjoyment every day and then throughout the year that is not part of being a teacher?
6. What professional task do you enjoy the least, or gives you anxiety, but you know it is necessary?
7. What strategies do you have or things you have done to ensure these tasks get done without becoming overwhelming?
8. What professional tasks do you enjoy the most?
   a. How do you balance these tasks with tasks that you do not find as enjoyable?
9. What advice do you have for a teacher in terms of time-management?
10. What advice do you have for a teacher in terms of self-care?

After you have completed the interview, go back and write down three to five suggestions or ideas that you now have for yourself. It can be specific suggestions that the teacher gave or it can be ideas that you now have that are based on the advice the teacher provided and which you did not consider. For example, the teacher might have shared information about what to do during lunch time that you did not even think about before the interview. Take a few minutes to jot down these ideas so you can keep them in mind as you construct your own self-care plan later in the chapter. Do not forget to write a thank-you note and share your appreciation to this teacher.

"TEACHER TALK": PRACTICAL STRATEGIES FROM EXPERIENCED TEACHERS

Teachers are fantastic resources. The following teacher talk comes from an experienced teacher who shares her advice and strategies for maintaining a personal and professional balance.

Teacher Talk 1

Self-Care. These two words spring up a slew of emotions for all of us, and especially for teachers. As teachers, our whole job is spent helping others, and we often care for ourselves last, if there is any energy or time left over. My personal ideas around self-care have changed a great deal during my twenty-year teaching career. Early on in my career, I thought I had to stay at school for four-plus hours after school everyday in order to be considered a competent teacher. Coming home exhausted after a twelve-hour plus day and often working more hours at home is not sustainable, but sometimes hard to avoid. I have developed some intentional self-care tips that I have learned and worked hard to apply over the years, in order to help me better manage my self-care:

1. I really aim to get at least seven hours of sleep a night. Sometimes I go to bed at 8:00 p.m. and get up early if I still need to get school work done; sometimes I go to bed at 10:00 p.m. and get up the next morning right before I need to leave. Regardless of how my work and sleep time may be structured, I really, really commit to getting at least seven hours of sleep every night. I believe we must be well rested in order to show up the best people we can for our students.
2. In the schools I have worked, there have been a variety of opportunities offered for teachers, within the school building, to help teachers in the area of self-care. For example, in one school where I worked, our school counselor was a certified yoga teacher; for the whole year, she offered weekly, after-school yoga classes for an hour on Thursdays in the school's music classroom. This class offered teachers a solid hour of yoga, rejuvenation, a time to connect with colleagues, and most importantly, an hour built into teachers' weeks that is just for them, in the school building. I have also worked in schools where a group of teachers decided they want to work out after school and together they did an online workout program, projected in a teacher's classroom on the SMARTBOARD or projector screen. At another school where I worked, a few of us were talking about how we enjoyed running, and we started our own "running club." Getting a workout done right after school without leaving the school building or school grounds is a great time-saver as well as a great social outlet.
3. Many school districts offer free counseling services for teachers and staff. My current school district offers eight free counseling sessions per academic year; these counseling sessions are very easy to set up for either in person or virtual counseling, which is matched to the teacher's needs.

4. I suggest setting a time to leave school each day; again as I said above, you do not have to stay late *every day* in order to be a great teacher! Some days you may want to stay late, but if some days you want to get outside, run an errand, meet a friend, do anything else, by all means *go and do that*, and know that the work can wait until a later time. Your time is valuable; you should aim to set boundaries about not working too late into the night and to not answer emails outside of set hours you determined. For example, my current principal recommended to us to try not answer emails outside the hours of 6:00 a.m. to 8:30 p.m.
5. As teachers, it seems like we have zero time in our school day and if we sit down for one minute, something else is not getting done and for this reason, I would just work through lunch break for years. Lately, I have found SO much value in getting out of my classroom during the lunch break, going into a shared space, and eating lunch with my colleagues. I think the time to connect with others (who are not your students) is invaluable. One thing I try to do in a forty-minute lunch break is to work for the first ten minutes in my classroom, then take fifteen to twenty minutes to eat and be with my colleagues, and then go back to the classroom ten minutes before the lunch break is over to prep for the afternoon. This way, I still feel like I am getting things done at lunch, but I am also making intentional time to connect with the people I work with and care about. I believe the mental benefits of taking a lunch break may exceed even the physical benefits.
6. Speaking of lunch, I believe that we cannot be our best teacher selves if we do not have on hand healthy snack options, lunch, and breakfast, and we stay hydrated. We are great at building in snack, lunch, and water break times for our kids; we should be doing the same for ourselves. I aim to prepare my breakfast, lunch, and snacks the night before. If you have access to a fridge or mini fridge at school, stock up on healthy snacks and drinks so they are accessible as you need. If your schools are like mine, there are always lots of treats in the staff room; it is nice to have your own healthy options on hand, so as to not give into all the temptations.
7. Lastly, I think self-care is also about taking more off your plate as a teacher and accepting help or delegate jobs to volunteers, paraprofessionals, or other staff members. Do not be afraid to ask for help and take someone up on their offer to help you! If this means not making a set of copies, someone else walking your students down to specials, or offering to help you with a student, be gracious and say *thank you*—you do not have to do it ALL! Trust me, you are already doing enough!

—*Teacher Amy Marvel*

Teacher Talk 2

When I was in college studying to be a teacher, I continuously heard the phrase, "Meredith, you need to learn how to say no." I ignored the comments about overcommitting myself and disregarded the feelings of anxiety that came as a result of this pattern. I struggled to find a balance between school work and personal life.

Like so many others, my life was turned upside down when the COVID-19 pandemic began in March 2020. My student teaching experience was quickly changed to teaching remotely in my childhood bedroom. Ripped away from my college, my student teaching classroom, and all of my friends, I became miserable and anxious. I thrived off having what I thought of as a "good routine" and suddenly, it was gone. However, being forced to slow down, take a breath, and change my routine led me to prioritize self-care as an educator.

During the COVID shutdown, I began to focus on my mental and physical health and quickly realized the benefit of making it a part of my routine. Whether it would be going on a walk, binge-watching a show, or practicing yoga, I blocked off time in my day when I would close my laptop and focus on myself. This newfound "me time" was life-changing. I realized that self-care would need to be a priority as I continued into my teaching career.

I recently started my third year of teaching. I believe that self-care has helped me become a better, happier teacher. I know that if I do not feel my best, I am not the best teacher for my students—and they deserve the best version of me.

In order to prioritize self-care, I set a schedule and a routine at the start of the week. To keep myself on track, I create a calendar outlining the type of exercise I should do each day. Not every week is perfect, but since self-care is a part of my daily routine, it is a priority just as much as my lesson plans and grading.

I have also accepted that as a teacher, my to-do list is never done. This has prevented me from staying after school for hours on end. When I feel myself becoming anxious about my overflowing to-do list I say to myself, "Am I prepared for tomorrow?" If the answer is yes, then I shut my laptop, leave my classroom, and make sure I "fill my tank" by practicing some form of self-care.

I encourage all teachers to carve out at least twenty minutes a day to do something for *you.* As teachers, we give love and attention to others constantly, but we can only continue to do that if we give love and attention to ourselves. I used to think, "Well I don't have twenty minutes." Now I think, "I *need* to have my twenty minutes"—and that mindset shift has changed everything.

—Teacher Meredith Miller

IT'S YOUR TURN: CREATE

We believe people become teachers because they want to work with students and they have a passion for creating learning experiences that will build students' love for learning and develop skills they need to participate in our global community. This is a big task, and teachers are up for it. However, sometimes novice teachers and the outsider's perspective do not see and understand the complexity of being a teacher with all of its elements and responsibilities that are part of the job. It is not just about instructional time, it is also about planning, grading, responding to concerned parents, monitoring and evaluating student academic and behavioral progress, being up to date on new pedagogical practices, knowing different curricula, understanding the community needs, and so much more. These additional tasks can be daunting and self-consuming. This is why it is imperative for teachers to pause and take time for themselves so they do not burnout.

In the following two activities you will start to think about your own self-care plan. You will begin by answering questions to learn more about yourself. You will then use that information to help construct a management plan that will work for you.

Create "Get to Know You"

You have read about a novice teacher and given her suggestions about ways to prioritize different professional tasks and make space for her personal life. You have heard from experienced teachers through the interview you conducted and reading the teacher talk section. Through these experiences you have heard from other teachers, and now it is time to take that information and start to think about what would and would not work for you.

Getting to know yourself when developing a self-care management plan is important. You can take advice and suggestions from others, but at the end of the day it must be a plan that works for you. In this activity, you will start to get to know yourself. There are four different sections: (1) General Questions, (2) Professional Tasks, (3) Confidence Level, and (4) Personal Inventory. Be honest as you go through each of these series of questions.

Once you have completed the questions, you will use this information to help construct your own self-care management plan in the next section.

Section 1: General Questions

Table 7.3. Self-Care General Questions

	Yes	No	I Don't Know / Maybe
I prefer to wake up early and do work in the morning.			
I prefer to do my work in the evening.			
I prefer to do all my work at school. I do not like to bring home any work.			
I prefer to be at school during the school hours and anything I do not get done during school hours I prefer to bring home and do at home on my own time.			
There are other personal responsibilities that I cannot change that prevent me from being able to stay at school to do work (i.e., childcare, pet, evening job, etc.).			

Section 2: Professional Tasks

Professional tasks must be accomplished. However, sometimes you can ask for help or share the responsibilities with colleagues or volunteers. For these questions, you are going to rate on a scale of 1 to 5 how much you enjoy the task (see table 7.4). 1 being you do not like it at all, and 5 being that it is one of your favorite professional tasks. Then for any item you gave a 3 or lower, you are going to write if this is a task you must do yourself, or is it a task that you could ask someone for help?

Table 7.4. Enjoyment Survey of Professional Tasks

	1	2	3	4	5	For tasks you scored 3 or lower, is it a task someone can help you accomplish (yes / no)? If yes, who might be able to help?
Lesson Planning: Reading						
Lesson Planning: Writing						
Lesson Planning: Science						
Lesson Planning: Math						
Lesson Planning: Social Studies						
Preparing Materials (i.e., making copies)						
Writing Newsletter						
Professional Development Activities						
Grading Student Work						

(continued)

Table 7.4. (continued)

	1	2	3	4	5	*For tasks you scored 3 or lower, is it a task someone can help you accomplish (yes / no)? If yes, who might be able to help?*
Input Student Grades and Report Cards						
Assessing Student Progress						
Bulletin Boards and Class Beautification						
Classroom Organization						
Respond to Parents (emails or phone calls)						

Section 3: Confidence Level

Confidence plays a big role when thinking about your self-care management plan. Oftentimes teachers are more confident in certain areas. Confidence or the lack of confidence can impact many things. For example, it might impact which tasks you decide to do first and which tasks you avoid. It might determine how much time you spend on a task. The following questions are designed to have you think about your confidence in planning, communicating with families, and your perception of how colleagues view you as a teacher. As you answer these questions, you want to think about your confidence and how it impacts these areas. It can influence what you do and how much time you spend on different professional tasks.

Questions about Planning:

- Do you feel confident planning and preparing lessons in ALL subject areas?
- Or do you feel more confident in some subjects, but not others?
- If so, about which subjects do you feel more confident, and which ones do you feel less confident?
- When you are not as confident in a subject area do you then take more time to plan because you want to get it just right, or do you try to avoid it and put it off until the end?

Questions about Communicating with Families

- Do you feel confident writing and sending home communication to families?
- Does it take you a longer time to email, or write a newsletter knowing that it must be written correctly?

- Do you like having parents help in the classroom?
- When parents or other volunteers come into your room to help, do you feel you are being watched and evaluated?

Questions about Colleagues

- Do you feel other teachers think you are a good teacher? Why or why not?
- Do you feel other teachers evaluate you?
- Do you feel the administration thinks you are a good teacher? Why or why not?
- What do you think your colleagues would say you do best? Why?
- What do you think your colleagues would say you need to work on? Why?

Section 4: Personal Inventory

Now that you have answered a variety of professional questions, it is time to think about personal responsibilities you have and the things you like to do for enjoyment. For this section, you will complete table 7.5. The first three columns are designed to have you think about the activities you do for fun or activities you would like to do. For example, the first column asks you to list activities you like to do on a daily basis. You might like to read on a daily basis, but right now you do not have time to do that. It is okay. You should still list it.

The objective is for you to discover and think about the types of activities you like to engage in or would like to try on a daily, weekly, monthly, and yearly basis. The four columns are for you to list all your personal responsibilities. These might be activities you also enjoy doing. For example, if you have a dog, you probably are responsible for walking the dog throughout the day. If you have children, you might need to list when you need to be available after school.

Table 7.5. Personal Activities Inventory

List activities you like to do on a daily basis	*List activities you like to do on a weekly or monthly basis*	*List activities you like to do throughout the year*	*List your personal responsibilities*

Now that you have completed listing activities, you will want to go back and circle the activities and responsibilities you actually do right now. By doing this, you will start to see which activities you currently do and have time to do. You will also start to see which activities you prioritize. Then go back and look at the items you have not circled. Put a star next to those items that you would like to prioritize and try to make space for in your schedule.

Create a Personal Self-Care Management Plan

Now that you have gone through the different activities in this chapter, it is time to apply them to yourself. Begin by writing your daily to-do list, and then prioritizing those items. Then write a typical daily schedule. Highlight events on the schedule that are required and the time is not flexible. Then in some other way, identify events that you need to do but the time is flexible.

Once you have mapped out everything, it is time for you to create a new dream daily schedule. You will take everything you have learned about yourself from this chapter and create a new daily schedule. You must keep the events that you highlighted and identified as required, but the rest you can move around. You need to include when you will accomplish different tasks from your to-do list. As you create this new daily schedule remember to write in activities that make you happy and give you enjoyment. Take inventory of your daily life and find ways to make it more manageable. Developing self-care techniques is essential for the balance of personal and professional wellness helping you so that you may have many years of successful classroom ballets.

REFERENCES

Armstrong, T. (2019). *Mindfulness in the classroom: Strategies for promoting concentration, compassion, and calm*. ASCD.

Fabbro, A., Fabbro, F., Capurso, V., D'Antoni, F., & Crescentini, C. (2020). Effects of mindfulness training on school teachers' self-reported personality traits as well as stress and burnout levels. *Perceptual and Motor Skills, 127*(3), 515–532.

Frank, J. L., Reibel, D., Broderick, P., Cantrell, T., & Metz, S. (2015). The effectiveness of mindfulness-based stress reduction on educator stress and well-being: Results from a pilot study. *Mindfulness, 6*(2), 208–216.

Garner, P. W., Bender, S. L., & Fedor, M. (2018). Mindfulness-based SEL programming to increase preservice teachers' mindfulness and emotional competence. *Psychology in the Schools, 55*(4), 377–390.

Jennings, P. A., Brown, J. L., Frank, J. L., Doyle, S., Oh, Y., Davis, R., . . . & Greenberg, M. T. (2017). Impacts of the CARE for Teachers program on teachers' social and emotional competence and classroom interactions. *Journal of Educational Psychology*, *109*(7), 1010.

Lucas, L. J. (2017). *Practicing presence*. Stenhouse Publishers.

Zarate, K., Maggin, D. M., & Passmore, A. (2019). Meta-analysis of mindfulness training on teacher well-being. *Psychology in the Schools*, *56*(10), 1700–1715.

www.ingramcontent.com/pod-product-compliance
Lightning Source LLC
Chambersburg PA
CBHW020806160426
43192CB00006B/466